What Have I Done?

A Victim Empathy Programme For Young People

Pete Wallis

with Clair Aldington and Marian Liebmann

Jessica Kingsley Publishers
London and Philadelphia

First published in 2010
by Jessica Kingsley Publishers
116 Pentonville Road
London N1 9JB, UK
and
400 Market Street, Suite 400
Philadelphia, PA 19106, USA

www.jkp.com

Library of Congress Cataloging in Publication Data
Wallis, Pete.
  What have I done? : a victim empathy programme for young people /
Pete Wallis, with Clair Aldington and Marian Liebmann.
     p. cm.
  Includes bibliographical references.
  ISBN 978-1-84310-979-2 (pb : alk. paper) 1. Restorative justice. 2. Juvenile delinquents--Psychology.
3. Victims of crimes. 4. Empathy. I. Aldington, Clair. II. Liebmann, Marian, 1942- III. Title.
  HV8688.W354 2010
  364.6'8--dc22
                                  2009019467

British Library Cataloguing in Publication Data
A CIP catalogue record for this book is available from the British Library

ISBN 978 1 84310 979 2

Printed and bound in Great Britain by
Athenaeum Press, Gateshead, Tyne and Wear

Contents

Figures

Acknowledgements

Special thanks to:

Aik Saath, Andrew Bates (Forensic Psychologist, Thames Valley Probation), Richard Beckett (Psychologist, Oxford Forensic Psychology Service), Catie Blundell (Restorative Justice Worker, Reading Youth Offending Service), Selma Rikberg-Smyly (Consultant Clinical Psychologist, Ridgeway NHS Trust, Oxford), Julie Morgan (Partner, KPMG LLP), Roger Cullen (Senior Policy Advisor on Restorative Justice, Youth Justice Board), the staff, volunteers and management of Oxfordshire Youth Offending Service, including Tan Lea, Vicki Smith, Joe Shears, Jane Fangman, Michelle Woods, Mark Webb, Mick Vockins, Emma Massingham, Gordon Richardson, Lesley Boylan and the young people who provided feedback as the exercises were piloted, Caroline Marrie Metcalf, Denise Cullingham, Vince Mercer (Co-ordinator, AIM Project), Howard Zehr (Professor of Restorative Justice, Centre for Justice and Peacebuilding, Eastern Mennonite University, US), Thalia Wallis, Marguerite Wallis, Sean McWeeney, Cathy Betoin, Elizabeth Clarkin (Northumbria Probation Service), Jane Bingham (Freelance writer for children and teenagers and Royal Literary Fund Fellow, Oxford Brookes University), Nicky Gunter (Newham Youth Offending Team), The Alternatives to Violence Project (AVP), Barbara Tudor (West Midlands Area Victim/Offender Development Officer, National Probation Service), Dr Belinda Hopkins (Director of Transforming Conflict, the National Centre for Restorative Justice in Youth Settings), Lindy Wootton (Restorative Justice Practitioner/Consultant, HMP Bristol Restorative Justice Project 2003–4), Remedi Victim Offender Mediation Service, Sheffield, Clare Honeysett (Senior Probation Officer, Thames Valley Probation), Kate Netten (Probation Officer, Thames Valley Probation), Harriet Bailey and the Restorative Justice Consortium, including attendees of the RJC Networking Day, October 2008, Gillian Riley (Victim Liaison Officer, Northumbria Probation Area), Hazel Kemshall, HMP Preston Restorative Justice Project, Shaun Kirkpatrick, Leicestershire Probation. With grateful thanks to Stephen Jones, Melanie Wilson and eveyone at Jessica Kingsley Publishers.

The authors apologize deeply if material is inadvertently borrowed from other sources without proper recognition.

The Conflict Tree exercise is reproduced with kind permission from Fisher, S. *et al.*(2000) *Working with Conflict: Skills and Strategies for Action.* London: Zed Books.

The Feelings Graphs exercises have been adapted with kind permission from Anne Rawlings (Editor) (1996) *Ways and Means.* London: Kingston Friends Mediation.

'Gains and losses', 'Telling it like it was', and 'My opinion, my values' have been adapted with kind permission from Nottinghamshire Probation Service's *Targets for Effective Change* manual.

Footprints graphic on p.182 adapted from the US Environmental Protection Agency's Getting in Step Programme (www.epa.gov/nps/toolbox/guide.htm).

The Victim Empathy Scale has been designed by Beckett, R.C. and Fisher, D.. Address for correspondence: Oxford Forensic Psychology Service, 17 Pipley Furlong, Oxford OX4 4JW.

This programme was written on behalf of Oxfordshire County Council.

The authors will be delighted to receive any feedback on how to improve this course and the exercises it contains. Please contact them via Jessica Kingsley Publishers by post at 116 Pentonville Road, London N1 9JB, or by email on post@JKP.com.

Section I:
Theoretical and Practical Background

Who is this workbook for?

This workbook is a practical guide to victim empathy work with young people who have offended, and can be used in an individual case-work setting or as a groupwork programme. The course can be delivered by case managers, group workers, volunteers, reparation or victim workers or other staff as appropriate in youth offending teams, young offender institutions, probation teams, restorative justice services or reparation programmes. The course may also be useful in schools, care homes, Connexions (information and advice service for young people), youthwork settings or in any other context where young people who have committed offences may benefit from a course in victim empathy.

Although designed to be run as a victim empathy course, it is a resource to draw on and build upon as appropriate, offering a range of exercises to use with different individuals. It is designed to be flexible and adaptable for use with young people of differing ages, offences, backgrounds and abilities. It recognizes that young people who offend have often experienced victimization themselves, and brings this into a number of the exercises.

Although designed for young people, the age and emotional development of older people who offend may not be so different, and the course may be suited for working in the adult system.

The course is designed for use with any type of offending where it is possible to identify a person or people who were affected (with the exception of domestic violence or sex offending – see section on 'Assessment for suitability' on p.19). The workbook hasn't been 'themed' by types of offences like some victim empathy courses. This doesn't imply that people who offend all share the same motivations or attitudes to offending, or that all those who have been victimized have the same reactions. You may find that certain exercises work better with offences of violence, for example, whilst others are more suited to property crime. The workbook can be used flexibly, bearing in mind that every offence, every person who has been hurt by crime and every person who offends is unique.

We have tried to use inclusive language throughout; the workbook is for use with male and female young people.

What is victim empathy?

What is empathy?

This course is designed to encourage empathy in young people who commit crimes. Empathy is a process of feeling for another person. Most people who commit crimes know at the time that their actions are wrong, and that someone else will be hurt. However they manage to close off those feelings and avoid thinking about the people whom they victimize. Victim empathy work helps them to acknowledge that it is real people that they have harmed. Empathy engenders a sense of shared experience, and an identification with and understanding of the other person's situation, feelings and motives. Empathy has the potential to profoundly change our interactions with one another.

Why is a victim empathy programme important for the young person who has offended?

Anyone who has worked with young people who have committed crimes will be familiar with a common inclination to minimize the consequences their actions have had on others, to shift the blame and to concentrate on their own feelings of victimization and hurt. These attempts to shut out difficult thoughts and feelings may be a natural (but mistaken) mechanism to help them feel worthwhile and good about themselves.

In contrast, those who have accompanied a young person through a restorative meeting (or indirect mediation) will have witnessed an approach that keeps the person who was hurt clearly in mind and at the centre of proceedings. If the restorative process has been successful the young person will have learnt about the impact of their behaviour and experienced empathy for those who were affected. They may develop improved self-control, higher self-esteem and better motivation as a result. They build greater intimacy in relationships and are able to resolve future conflicts restoratively, potentially leading to reduced re-offending. They may come out of the experience feeling better and happier about themselves.

Working on developing victim empathy can be helpful when exploring, preparing for and supporting a restorative approach, or as a stand alone exercise if more direct restorative avenues aren't available (see section on 'Victim empathy and the restorative process' on p.13). In common with the restorative process, empathy has three elements, which must be included in any victim awareness programme. The first element involves cognition (thinking) and the ability to perceive cognitively the perspective of another person. The second element involves affect (feeling), and the ability to recognize the emotions and feelings that this produces within oneself. The third element involves behaviour (doing) and the ability to respond appropriately and with compassion, motivated by those feelings and thoughts.

Encouraging empathy for those they hurt allows the young person to reflect on the harm their behaviour has caused to others, and challenges them to consider what might be done to try to repair some of that harm.

We should remember however that the expression of empathy is a social construct. Each individual will experience and express empathy differently. Empathy is also subject to environment influences; to assess a young person's victim empathy whilst they are in a stressful custodial setting is unlikely to give the same indication as a similar exercise in the community. The expression of empathy for others will differ with young people depending on their personality, their backgrounds, their life experience and their culture. There may be young people who are not ready to start this work, and for whom a course in emotional literacy may be a necessary precursor (see 'Assessment for suitability' on p.19).

With all these issues in mind, this course is based on the premise that realizing how our behaviour affects others is a vital part of growing up. It asserts that empathy is something that can be worked on and that young people are open to change, even if the steps are small.

It could be said that we are all 'offenders' to some degree. We all inevitably cause hurt at some stage of our lives and perhaps there are suggestions here for everyone. Causing hurt, in spite of the fact that we try not to, is universal and the strategies the young people learn on this programme may stand them in good stead throughout their lives.

How does victim empathy relate to guilt, shame and remorse?

Some young people who have committed an offence will genuinely say that they are ashamed of their actions, and when asked, a surprising number do wish to know about how the people they hurt are feeling. However many if not most people who commit a crime will seek to avoid difficult feelings of shame and self-blame by avoiding thinking about the negative effects of their actions on others. This course seeks to identify and challenge their defensive thinking mechanisms which may include denial, minimization, blaming the victim and denial of self-control.

As the young person progresses through this course and is encouraged to take on board difficult information about the wide-ranging effects of their actions, they may start to feel shame. There has been a lot of debate about whether shame per se is helpful. John Braithwaite introduced the concept of reintegrative shaming.[1] He asserted that if shame is stigmatic the result is likely to be negative, whilst shame that doesn't stigmatize is a healthy emotion, as long as the person can retain their dignity. Perhaps the key in victim empathy work is when the young person experiences being ashamed of what they have *done*, not of them*selves*. This can be a positive sign, and one which shows that they are starting to think about other people. It can be a first step to them becoming reintegrated or welcomed back into their community.

Whilst this course isn't specifically designed to invoke shame, the young person may feel ashamed and remorseful as they move through the exercises. It is important to keep an eye on how deep these feelings are being experienced, and

---

1   Braithwaite, J. (1989) *Crime, Shame and Reintegration.* Cambridge: Cambridge University Press.

to remind the young person of their many positive gifts and attributes if they are becoming disheartened.

The course moves on from a greater understanding of the impact of the offence towards exploring opportunities for the young person to consider how to repair the harm they have caused. It is hoped that this course will leave the young person with a renewed sense of their own worth, having learnt about how their behaviour affects others, both negatively through crime and positively through their own efforts towards reparation.

How does the course acknowledge the social and environmental context that leads to crime rather than focusing solely on blaming the individual?

A criticism of John Braithwaite's theory of reintegrative shaming has been that it focuses on the individual responsibility of the person who has offended, without acknowledging the complex social and environmental causes of crime. In this workbook, some of the exercises are designed to help the young person to explore the root causes of their offending. Experience shows that young people can readily identify the wider influences that have contributed to their crimes, from peer pressure, lack of opportunities, prejudices, easy access to alcohol, poor role models etc. This knowledge may help the case worker to consider how best to address these offence-related needs.

Victim empathy and reparation

Victim empathy sessions could be used for the first few sessions of a young person's reparation programme, and can be a helpful way to identify the more practical reparation task that the young person would like to do to pay back for their offence. In each case, ensure that there is communication with your agency's Reparation Team to alert them to any reparation related issues arising from this course, and make referrals where appropriate.

Victim empathy and the restorative process

Victim empathy work can be done in parallel with any direct or indirect restorative work being explored individually with the young person, and may indeed be used as part of the preparation for a restorative process. Many of the exercises in the workbook draw upon the young person's own experience, and can include information coming in (e.g. from a restorative justice or victim worker) about the real life impact of their offence on those they hurt.

The final module looks at ways of repairing the harm caused. If there hasn't been an opportunity for a restorative process prior to this, the exercises may lead to a letter to, or an expressed wish to meet the people they hurt or desire to make good through reparation which might kick-start a restorative process (providing the other party is interested). The person who was victimized may like to learn about the work that the young person has been engaged in, and the material the young person produces during this course could be turned into a 'show and tell' presentation. This could, where appropriate, involve a 'surrogate victim'[2] and/or the young person's parents, carers or case worker.

Victim empathy work should never be seen as an alternative to exploring the potential for face-to-face or indirect contact in a restorative approach, unless and until all avenues for restorative work have been exhausted. Victim empathy work cannot be described as a restorative approach unless there is a direct benefit to those who were affected by the crime and some form of communication between the parties.

However, it can be the case that the aggrieved person would like to be involved, but that the young person is showing little remorse or understanding. Victim empathy work can be used effectively to unlock the potential for a more fruitful restorative encounter at a later stage.

If those who were hurt aren't involved at all, perhaps because it hasn't been physically possible to establish contact with them, victim empathy work is better than nothing.

Restorative principles and values

Regardless of whether the young person is engaged in a restorative process, the victim empathy programme should be delivered in accordance with restorative principles and values. Drawing on the axiom *'if you don't model what you are teaching then you are teaching something else'*, it is critically important for the delivery of the programme itself to model the restorative approach. Restorative values informing this workbook include:

- respectful relationships

- a belief in everyone's ability to find their own solutions

- honesty and openness

---

2   A 'surrogate victim' is someone who has been the victim of a crime, who is later invited to meet people who have committed crimes against others to share and discuss their experience. It will always be more powerful for there to be a more direct restorative meeting between the person who committed the crime and those they hurt, but this may not always be possible. Involving a 'surrogate victim' can be an effective second best. Care is required to avoid 'using' crime victims for the benefit of the criminal justice system (although they will, it is hoped, find the experience helpful), and it may be best for 'surrogate victims' to be involved only once or twice so that they can put their experience behind them.

- taking responsibility

- active listening, sensitive checking and exploration of meanings

- an open and non-judgemental approach that avoids taking sides

- a commitment to empowering and developing confidence in others

- inclusion and acceptance of diversity

- care with the ownership of information.

The course includes exercises that may help to identify your own and the young person's core values and beliefs. You are encouraged to explore these values together and make them explicit, leading to Follow-up Exercise 4.8: The Martians have landed! on p.178.

It can be helpful to negotiate with the young person how you would both like your working relationship to be (see 'Expectations' on p.33). Be open about your own expectations and commitment.

Terminology

Although this workbook uses the term 'victim empathy', try to avoid using the word 'victim' as a noun with the young person where possible. The danger is that it implies that the experience of victimhood is the sole feature of the person who was hurt, rather than one aspect of their lives. Encourage the use of the person's real name if it is known. If not, you could consider choosing a fictitious name (n.b. see the subsection on 'Confidentiality' on p.18).

This pack attempts to avoid referring directly to 'the victim', speaking instead about 'the person who was hurt during the offence'. This is intended to be a general catch-all for any person who was affected, whether physically, emotionally or materially by the offence. The workbook also tends to refer to one main person who was hurt, but this can be translated into two or more if there is more than one 'primary victim'.

Notes for facilitators

The course is designed to be used on an individual basis or as a groupwork programme, and instructions are given for both settings. In some youth justice settings it will be the young person's individual case manager who will deliver the course, often as part of a supervision plan on a community order or prevention programme. In other situations the course will be delivered by a different member of the team, such as a groupwork facilitator, victim liaison officer, reparation worker, education worker, etc. In a school, Connexions, youthwork or children's home setting, the young person may not have a case manager as such, although there may still be a key worker.

For the sake of simplicity, this course will refer to the person, or persons in the context of groupwork, delivering the material in this workbook as the 'facilitator'. If the young person also has a case manager or key worker (who is not the course facilitator), it will be vital for there to be good communication, so that the case manager or key worker learns about and can build upon the significant work that the young person engages in during the course.

The effects on you as a facilitator

Victim empathy work can be a challenging and stressful part of your engagement with a young person. In more serious cases the young person will require substantial support as they explore the full extent of the harm they have caused to other people. It is therefore important to establish a good working relationship with the young person in order to embark on victim empathy work. Young people who offend have often experienced victimization as well, and the memory of a young person's own victim experience can be used to enhance an empathic understanding of the harm they may have caused to others, providing this is approached sensitively.[3]

Guidance notes for facilitators

As you work on victim empathy with your clients:

- Remember that it is empowering for the young person to know that they can help.

- Congratulate the young person for being willing to confront difficult emotions.

- Talk about disclosure/confidentiality and establish appropriate boundaries.

- Consider referrals to mental health or counselling services where appropriate.

- Make use of your own supervision.

- Contact your victim/restorative justice team for advice.

---

3 The Edinburgh Study explored the 'victim offender overlap', establishing that the experience of being victimized at a young age frequently correlates with offending at a later stage, and that offending at an early age also correlates with becoming victimized later on. It isn't uncommon to have the same young person appearing in court as a victim, witness and offender at different times.

Look for signs that the young person is becoming distressed by the exercises. Direct signs of distress may include:

- changes in usual behaviour

- anger and/or hostility

- tearfulness

- being very quiet and withdrawn

- disruptive behaviour

- difficulty concentrating and /or completing work

- being missing from the individual or group sessions.

Be prepared to be flexible and ready to drop exercises if they are becoming too distressing. You may choose to introduce a game or activity that is less challenging or suggest a break. In groupwork settings one of the facilitators can provide individual support for a client who is showing signs of distress. Be sure to discuss these issues during feedback after the group and agree any ongoing needs that should be followed up.

- Throughout this programme of work, be sensitive to the young person's own experiences, encouraging them to only disclose what they feel comfortable with, particularly in relation to any experiences of victimization they have had themselves.

- Be cautious when engaging the young person in considering a situation when they have been the victim of an offence or situation. This can encourage the young person to see themselves as a 'victim', making it difficult to shift their thinking towards the impact that their behaviour will have had on others.

- Be careful about disclosure of further offending which these exercises may bring out. If you have any concerns – discuss with your supervisor.

- Avoid colluding with the young person, by reinforcing any minimization or denial they may express about their offence. Without talking with the person who was hurt, it is impossible to predict the impact of an offence, and many so called 'minor' crimes can be devastating for the person hurt.

Remember that some young people may say what they think they are supposed to say rather than what they really feel. This is for you as their facilitator to assess and monitor.

EXPECTATIONS

Establish agreed expectations (i.e. ground rules) at the start, ideally eliciting these from the participants (see 'Expectations: What I need to work well' on p.33). You might also consider a contract that is signed during the pre-course interview. Reinforce the importance of everyone arriving on time, including the facilitators.

HEALTH AND SAFETY

Remember any necessary health and safety announcements, and consider issues such as access to toilets, smoking or refreshment breaks, fire escapes and your own safety as facilitators. You may also need to consider health and safety implications and carry out risk assessments for any art materials and/or equipment you choose to use. Try to find a room that is pleasant and conducive to groupwork or one-to-one work which will not be interrupted or disturbed by noise.

CONFIDENTIALITY

Confidentiality usually won't be an issue when using the workbook individually with a young person. In a groupwork setting, however, participants will be curious to learn about each others' offences. They are encouraged to share details of what happened and the effect on themselves and those they hurt. It may be best to avoid and discourage detailed disclosure where it might identify other parties, in case they are known to other group members. Discuss and agree confidentiality during preparation and at the start of the group.

CONSISTENCY

Try to create consistency throughout the course and during each session, by having the same start and end times for example, and by establishing clear expectations and boundaries. In a groupwork setting, you could create consistency by using Circle Time to begin and end each session.

BREAKS AND REFRESHMENTS

Consider offering healthy food and drink during the group session (some young people may turn up hungry, and low blood sugar levels can lead to disruptive behaviour) and decide whether it will be helpful to have a break.

Guidance notes for managers

The exercises contained within this workbook are designed to be immediately accessible for experienced facilitators to use with their clients. However victim empathy work is challenging, and the authors recommend that appropriate training and supervision be made available to ensure that facilitators are well supported in delivering this course, and to encourage consistency of delivery. Consider options for generic groupwork training if there isn't anything more specific available.

Assessment for suitability

Victim empathy work is intended to be challenging; to move the young person towards being able to see the effects of their actions on other real people and feel empowered to do something about it.

A pre-course interview is likely to be the main tool in determining the suitability of applicants. This course isn't tailored for use with domestic violence or sex offences, in which issues around victim empathy, denial and acceptance of responsibility as well as shame and blame are usually more complex and sensitive. Otherwise the only reason someone should be excluded from taking any of the modules would be if they totally deny committing an offence ('*I wasn't there*'). Partial acceptance of responsibility is not necessarily a problem ('*I didn't do what they said, but I did do something*' or '*I was there but I didn't do anything*'). Be clear about the purpose and requirements of the course with the young person.

There may be some young people, perhaps those who have had particularly traumatic and unsupported upbringings, who may need to do some initial work on emotional literacy before they can empathize with others. A young person locked in rage through unmet needs may not be able to engage and show remorse. For these young people, pacing the victim empathy work will be key – they will need to feel safe enough to allow themselves to feel shame, and yet know that they can still feel accepted and respected. Their relationship with their case worker is important in supporting this process. If the course is being delivered by a different professional, the case worker should be kept informed. Perhaps they could be invited in to share the experience at the final session, and at other key points in the programme. If the situation at home is working against the victim empathy agenda (with parent(s)/carer(s) locked in denial or finger pointing, for example), it may make sense to involve the parent(s)/carer(s) in the programme, or inform them about this work. For some young people, working on victim empathy may come later in their programme, if at all.

Prior to commencing the Modules and after the programme, the young person will complete the 'Pre- and post-victim empathy scales' (see p.195). In addition, you can link this assessment to your own organization's restorative justice assessment framework for restorative interventions, to assess the young person's suitability for engagement in direct or indirect restorative processes.

If there is a strong indication that direct or indirect restorative processes are applicable and the young person is already showing genuine remorse and victim empathy, this course can be used to prepare for or reinforce those processes. Victim empathy work helps restorative work.

If there is a delay in contacting the person who was hurt, or if the young person is showing little remorse, the course can be used to prepare them for a potential restorative process later on.

Always prioritize restorative interventions over victim empathy work.

Groupwork

All of the exercises in *What Have I Done?* contain instructions for use in groupwork settings as well as during individual supervision. This course has been run successfully both with individuals and in groups, with good results, although careful selection and preparation of clients are crucial (see 'Preparation' below). A good group can lead to helpful dynamics between clients which may challenge, encourage, open up and support the participants in ways that may not be achieved in individual work. On the other hand, it may feel more appropriate for the case worker to explore this sensitive area individually as an integrated part of the young person's programme.

It may also make sense to arrange for some of the victim empathy work to be done in a group, with other parts completed individually.

Good groupwork practice
PREPARATION

Preparation for groupwork is essential, both in planning each session and in the selection of participants. It may be helpful for potential group members to have completed some prior work on offending behaviour with the facilitator or another professional involved in their case, and to have a chance to talk about the group before it starts. This preparation will establish their willingness and ability to engage in victim empathy work and avoid a situation where one individual who isn't ready wrecks the group for everyone else. Simply turning up to the group is only half of the commitment they need to make.

Although a perfect balance may not be practicable, try to avoid a situation in which one person might feel isolated because they are the only girl, are much younger than the rest, are from a different background, are at a different stage in their offending career or have committed a very different offence, etc. Conduct pre-course interviews with prospective participants to establish suitability, being mindful of the mix of clients, readiness to engage, maturity and attitude to their offence and the person they hurt.

Including participants who have committed different offences can work well, as people may experience similar feelings, but it may be worth considering running separate groups for property offences and offences against the person. Oxfordshire Youth Offending Service has run a series of successful 'Assault Awareness' courses for young people who have committed violent offences, incorporating a visit to Accident & Emergency (see Follow-up exercise 2.5 on p.117). Similar groups could run for car offences, burglaries, criminal damage or retail theft, etc.

ICE-BREAKERS AND WARM-UP GAMES

Ice-breaking and warm-up games and exercises can help in the development of a positive group dynamic, build and establish rapport between participants, bring variety and provide welcome relief when dealing with challenging materials. Some of the exercises contained in this course can be used as ice-breakers, but it may be worth exploring other ideas. There are lots of books with group games and exercises, including:

> *Winners All: Co-operatives Games for All Ages* (Anon, illustrated by Ann Clark). Published by Pax Christi (1980).

> *Let's Play Together* (Mildred Masheder). Published by Green Print (1991).

> *Games, Games, Games* (Unknown author). Published by The Woodcraft Folk (1998).

> *The Gamesters' Handbook 3* (Donna Brandes). Published by Trans-Atlantic Publications (1998).

> *Playing with Fire: Training in the Creative Use of Conflict* (Nic Fine and Fiona Macbeth). Published by the National Youth Agency in the UK and New Society Publishers in USA and Canada (1992).

Always have more ideas and exercises than you are likely to need, so that you have something up your sleeve if a particular exercise doesn't work, or if you find that the group is moving through the programme faster than anticipated. Flexibility is a key skill in groupwork facilitation.

CIRCLE TIME

This is a restorative process in frequent use in schools and residential settings. The idea of seating people in a circle helps everyone to feel of equal importance, and allows each participant to make eye contact with everyone else in the group. A circle is inclusive, presents a level playing field and has no beginning or end. You may even consider having a round carpet or rug to emphasize the circle. Circle Time (you may choose to call it something different to avoid connotations of primary school) is a helpful way to start and end each session. You can use an object as a 'conch' or talking piece (for example a juggling ball) which is passed from person to person round the circle. Establish with the group that whoever has the object can talk without interruption. Give participants permission to 'pass' without speaking (and explain that this is fine). Check with those who passed at the end to see if they now wish to contribute.

You can suggest a topic for people to speak about round the circle, such as, 'Share something you have learnt today.' At the beginning of each module, we have made suggestions for Circle Time topics, but feel free to choose your own.

GROUP DYNAMICS

Much has been written elsewhere about the stages that groups pass through, and the different roles that participants can adopt as the group dynamic develops. Victim empathy groupwork is no different. Groupwork with young people who offend can start with participants testing the boundaries by seeing what they can get away with. It may become tempting to be shy of using the more demanding exercises in this workbook. Whilst it is important to adapt the course to the level and capacity of the group, don't take the easy route by avoiding using material that challenges the participants. We are attempting to bring change, potentially leading clients from denial, through shame to responsibility. Experience has shown that young people are able to grapple with difficult feelings and material, and even value the opportunity to talk about issues that may be on their minds.

It is important to avoid a situation where participants leave the group feeling burdened, or still in role following a role-play exercise. Finishing a session with something upbeat and practical that brings them back to the present can help. Given the nature of the topic, it might be wise to have at least one facilitator with good experience of groupwork.

Course structure

The course consists of four modules. These have been designed to follow the same pattern as a restorative meeting, which starts by considering the young person's story, moves on to the story of the person they hurt, considers who else has been affected and finally what can be done to repair the harm. However each module could stand alone if it isn't possible for individuals to complete each session in order.

This course can be adapted to the learning styles and needs of the participants, and includes exercises and options that require no reading or writing. Most of the material is intended to initiate and encourage discussion, although if a young person prefers to express themselves through writing there is plenty of scope for the exercises to be developed into written tasks. There are also worksheets for the young person which you may photocopy. The young person will need additional help and guidance. The work can be done directly onto the worksheets, but the participant may prefer to work on blank paper, or make use of different media (such as larger paper, art materials or a computer). A folder is useful for the young person to keep all the materials together.

Module 1: Thinking about what I did.

Module 2: Thinking about the person I hurt.

Module 3: Thinking about who else I affected.

Module 4: My chance to put things right.

Each module has a theme, which is explored in depth through a core exercise. There are lead-in exercises that can be used before the core exercise, and follow-up exercises to reinforce the core message. Some of the exercises have extension exercises to develop the theme; others have alternative exercises which may suit participants favouring artwork or who have literacy issues. Pick, choose and adapt the exercises to suit the specific needs of each client.

Clearly this resource is designed to be flexible, and care will be required when using it to plan a victim empathy course. It is not anticipated that the facilitator will work through every exercise in each module, but that they will pick and choose exercises that they think will work best for the individual or group. It isn't easy to anticipate how many of the exercises to include in one session or how participants will respond to a task, although it is always best to plan in more material than is likely to be required. There will be a period of trial and error for the facilitator when using the material for the first time, but approximate timescales are given for each exercise in the workbook.

Although this workbook is intended for building a victim empathy course, single exercises can be picked out and used on their own, or integrated with other material (for example from an offending behaviour or anger management course) by the experienced practitioner.

Although there are four modules, this doesn't restrict the programme to four sessions. In some settings it may make sense to have longer sessions (with breaks) in the morning and/or afternoons, and the course could then be completed within a week or two. In other contexts it can work well for the course to be run on a weekly basis; for example as a six-week course run on the same day and time every week. After school or early evenings are often the most convenient times.

Structure of each module

Lead-in exercises.

Core exercise.

Follow-up exercises.

Close and evaluation.

Lead-in exercises are intended to initiate discussion and engagement, and to prepare participants for the core message of the module. It isn't anticipated that every lead-in exercise will be used, but that the facilitator will choose ones they feel confident with and which suit the individual or group. Some lead-in or follow-up exercises can build on the theme of a previous exercise, but it is not necessary to have completed the previous exercise for it to work or have value.

The core exercise carries the central message of the module, and it is anticipated that these will be used each time the course is run.

Follow-up exercises deepen the discussion and reinforce the message of the core exercise, and again, it isn't anticipated that all will be used. Pick those that suit the participants, perhaps using exercises that are varied to maintain interest.

At the end of each session, ask the participant(s) to fill in the evaluation questionnaire on p.194. This will not only help the young person to think about what they have learned, it will also help you to run the course more smoothly and effectively next time.

Many of the exercises have suggestions on how they can be extended. These extension exercises may be useful if participants are responding well to a particular exercise and the facilitator feels that they can get more out of it, or if the initial exercise takes less time than planned. They may also offer more scope, for example for introducing the creative arts, or arranging a visit to a hospital or the crime scene.

The course is intended as a journey, not the building up of a portfolio, and often it is the discussion provoked by the exercises that is important. For some young people simply picking up a pen is a turn-off, so be as creative as possible with the use of different media and through the creative arts. Some of the exercises involve drawing, and there are suggestions in the workbook for further exploration of the themes through artwork. It is hoped that individual facilitators will feel empowered to experiment with different art media, and partnerships with local creative artists and art projects to enhance this work can also be explored. It may be possible to make creative use of technology, for example with a smart board (which is an interactive white board) on which the work can be called up and stored.

Many victim empathy courses make use of scenarios, case studies and news stories. This can be a helpful way in for the young person and material gathered, perhaps from the day's newspapers, can usefully be incorporated into many of the exercises. Where relevant additional material can be used to enhance an exercise this is clearly indicated.

Homework

Although the materials in this workbook are designed to be delivered directly to an individual or group, there is scope for some of the exercises to be set as homework. Homework can be used to reinforce the messages contained in the course, or to prepare for the next session. Some of the exercises can be developed through the creative arts, which could be worked on between sessions. Exercises that are potentially suitable for homework are indicated.

Given the often challenging nature of groupwork in youth justice settings, homework is not strongly recommended in this context, although it may work depending on the nature of the group. Difficulties may arise if it is not completed, if it is only achieved by some, and if the facilitator doesn't have time to read the homework or assess it before the feedback or discussion around it. It may be best to avoid a difficult dynamic and focus on the content of the group sessions.

Setting homework may be more successful with an individual programme, and the facilitator can judge whether or not it is likely to be completed. It is particularly recommended that the letter to the person I hurt (see p.158) is worked on between sessions, allowing the young person a chance to think about what they wish to say, and try various drafts in their own time.

Example timetables, structures and timings

Example one-to-one timetable

This example timetable is based on four one-to-one sessions of one hour. Timings are approximate and will depend on the individual's responsiveness, literacy skills, etc.

Session 1	Expectations: What I need to work well	10 mins
	Lead-in Exercise 1.1: My opinion, my values	10 mins
	Module 1 Core Exercise: Telling it like it was	15 mins
	Follow-up Exercise 1.7: DVD and discussion	10 mins
	Setting homework task	10 mins
	Close and evaluation	5 mins

Homework: Follow-up Exercise 1.6: What have I gained, what have I lost?

Session 2	Reminder of previous week	5 mins
	Homework feedback and discussion	5 mins
	Lead-in Exercise 2.1: Me as a victim	10 mins
	Module 2 Core Exercise: What's it like being the person I hurt?	15 mins
	Follow-up Exercise 2.3: A feelings graph for the person I hurt	10 mins
	Follow-up Exercise 2.4: DVD and discussion	10 mins
	Close and evaluation and setting homework	5 mins

Homework: Follow-up Exercise 2.2: What has the person I hurt gained and lost?

Session 3	Reminder of previous week	5 mins
	Homework feedback and discussion	5 mins
	Lead-in Exercise 3.1: Ripples	5 mins
	Module 3 Core Exercise: The ripples from my crime	10 mins
	Follow-up Exercise 3.1: Role play as my parent/carer	10 mins
	Follow-up Exercise 3.3: A feelings graph for my parent(s)/carer(s)	10 mins
	Follow-up Exercise 3.4: DVD and discussion	10 mins
	Close and evaluation and setting homework	5 mins

Homework: Starting on Follow-up Exercise 4.1: Letter to the person I hurt.

Session 4	Reminder of previous week	5 mins
	Module 4 Core Exercise: Crime tears people apart – what can help to put them back together?	20 mins
	Finishing Follow-up Exercise 4.1: Letter to the person I hurt	20 mins
	Follow-up Exercise 4.4: DVD and discussion	10 mins
	Close and evaluation	5 mins

Example groupwork timetable

This example timetable is based on six weekly sessions of one hour with a small group of five or six young people. If the group only meets at fortnightly or monthly intervals it may lose momentum and have less impact. Timings are approximate and depend on the group – always have extra exercises up your sleeve just in case.

Session 1	Circle Time: *'Your name and your favourite food'*	10 mins
	Expectations: What I need to work well	10 mins
	Lead-in Exercise 1.1: My opinion, my values	10 mins
	Module 1 Core Exercise: Telling it like it was	15 mins
	Circle Time: *'Something you are looking forward to'*	10 mins
	Close and evaluation	5 mins

Session 2	Reminder of previous week	5 mins
	Circle Time: '*A perfect day*'	10 mins
	Follow-up Exercise 1.3: How responsible am I for what happened?	10 mins
	Module 2 – Core Exercise: What's it like being the person I hurt?	15 mins
	Follow-up Exercise 2.4: DVD and discussion	10 mins
	Circle Time: '*Something you do well*'	5 mins
	Close and evaluation	5 mins
Session 3	Module 2 – Follow-up Exercise 2.5: Visit to A & E	1 hour
Session 4	Circle Time: '*What I learnt from last week*'	10 mins
	Reminder of previous week	5 mins
	Module 3 Core Exercise: The ripples from my crime	15 mins
	Module 3 Core Exercise: The ripples from my crime extension exercise – creating the ripple effect with the group	10 mins
	Follow-up Exercise 3.2: What has my family gained and lost?	10 mins
	Circle Time: '*Your favourite animal and why*'	5 mins
	Close and evaluation	5 mins
Session 5	Reminder of previous week	5 mins
	Circle Time: Sharing homework and discussion	10 mins
	Lead-in Exercise 4.1: My conflict tree	10 mins
	Follow-up Exercise 2.1: Being the person I hurt	10 mins
	Module 4 Core Exercise: Crime tears people apart – what can help to put them back together? Alternative exercise	15 mins
	Circle Time: '*Your favourite colour and why*'	5 mins
	Close and evaluation	5 mins

Homework: Starting on Follow-up exercise 4.1: Letter to the person I hurt.

Session 6	Reminder of previous week	5 mins
	Circle Time: *'What I learnt from last week'*	5 mins
	Follow-up Exercise 4.3: Persuade the person I hurt	10 mins
	Follow-up Exercise 4.5: My harmony tree	10 mins
	Follow-up Exercise 4.9: Looking to the future	10 mins
	Follow-up Exercise 4.9: Looking to the future extension exercise – if you have children, what do you hope they will be when they grow up?	10 mins
	Close and evaluation	5 mins
	Discussion about the course	5 mins

Homework: Complete Follow-up Exercise 4.1: Letter to the person I hurt (do this with case worker). Please see notes on groupwork in 'Homework' section (p.24)

Partnership with the case worker(s)

Often the case workers for group participants will be meeting with their clients between group sessions. Their support and partnership is crucial. Provide detailed feedback after each session so that the work can be reinforced during and after the groupwork programme. Consider whether some aspects of the course might best be covered by the case worker rather than in the group.

Useful organizations

Aik Saath Conflict Resolution Group
www.aiksaath.com

Leap Confronting Conflict
www.leaplinx.com

Transforming Conflict
www.transformingconflict.org

Restorative Justice Consortium, UK
www.restorativejustice.org.uk

Restorative Justice Online
www.restorativejustice.org

Youth Justice Board
www.yjb.gov.uk

Further reading

Cantacuzino, M. and Moody, B. (2004) *The F Word: Images of Forgiveness*. London: The Forgiveness Project. Also: www.theforgivenessproject.com

Crosland, P. and Liebmann, M. (eds) (2003) *40 Cases: Restorative Justice and Victim-Offender Mediation*. Bristol: Mediation UK. Now out of print but available on: www.restorativejustice.pbwiki.com/

Graef, R. (2001) *Why Restorative Justice?* London: Calouste Gulbenkian Foundation.

Johnstone, G. (2002) *Restorative Justice: Ideas, Values, Debates*. Cullompton: Willan.

Liebmann, M. (2007) *Restorative Justice: How It Works*. London: Jessica Kingsley Publishers.

Restorative Justice Consortium (2004) *Principles of Restorative Processes*. Available at www.restorativejustice.org.uk/?Resources:Best_Practice:Principles, accessed 27 October 2009.

Zehr, H. (2002) *The Little Book of Restorative Justice*. Intercourse, PA: Good Books (Can be ordered from London Mennonite Centre, tel: 020 8340 8775 or www.menno.org.uk/).

Section II:
Getting Started

Pre- and post-victim empathy scales

Encourage the young person to complete the Pre- and post-victim empathy scales on p.194. There is one scale for crimes of violence (VES(V)) and one for property crimes (VES(P)).

The same set of questions is asked before the course starts and after it is completed to measure any change in attitude. The initial results can be used to gauge the level of empathy the young person has before you commence victim empathy work. It may increase your understanding of where they are coming from and indicate areas of concern. This insight can inform your planning for the course.

The questionnaires are completed again at the end of the course. The results (comparing the 'before' and 'after') can be used in sentence plan reviews or evaluations to inform risk assessments, providing you have the young persons' consent. They can also indicate whether the course is of benefit and whether what you are offering in the course works in effecting change.

Remember that empathy is a slippery concept, and one that is difficult to define and measure. A young person may be able to empathize with people who have been victimized in other circumstances, but not in the context of their own offence. The validity of these scales will also depend on how well the young person can understand and answer the questions.

After you have run the scales with 20 or more young people you will have a good sense of a 'norm' for new young people coming into your service and a 'gold standard' for what you hope to achieve with participants on the course.

These victim empathy questionnaires and scales are reprinted with kind permission from Richard Beckett (Consultant Clinical Forensic Psychologist) and Dawn Fisher (Consultant Clinical Forensic Psychologist).

Instructions

For the Victim Empathy Scale for Violence (VES(V)) say to the young person and prepare a top sheet which says:

> I want you to think about what happened with [name the person who was victimized, or describe them, such as 'the boy at school' or 'the girl at the party'] and answer this questionnaire.

For the Victim Empathy Scale for Property (VES(P)) say to the young person and prepare a top sheet which says:

> Think about the person whose property was involved, and answer this questionnaire.

Show the young person how to put a cross through or circle the answer they are choosing on the scale. Deliver the instructions in a matter of fact way, and don't lead them to particular answers.

You may have to give more guidance, and possibly read out the questionnaire if the young person has literacy issues.

Expectations

What I need to work well

AIM

To establish agreed expectations between the young person (or for the group in a groupwork setting) and the facilitator.

APPROXIMATE TIME

5–10 mins

EQUIPMENT REQUIRED

- flipchart
- flipchart paper
- large Post-it™ notes
- coloured pens
- sticky spots or a marker pen

HANDOUTS NEEDED

This exercise is concerned with setting and agreeing ground rules for the duration of the course. However, it may feel more inclusive to use the phrase 'expectations' rather than 'ground rules'. The expectations could be visually displayed during each session so that they can be referred to if things go off track. By having this visual proof of what has been agreed at the outset, you can avoid possible confrontation later on.

Instructions

IN A ONE-TO-ONE SETTING

1. Give the young person four or five Post-it notes and ask them to write down on each Post-it one thing that they need to work well during this course. Give them a few examples to start them off, such as 'a quiet, tidy space' or 'being honest'.

2. In the meantime do the exercise yourself, writing down on Post-its your own expectations for the sessions, focusing on what you feel will be most helpful to get the best out of the course. You might like to refer to the sections at the start of this workbook, 'Notes for facilitators' on p.15 and 'Restorative principles and values' on p.14.

3. Ask the young person to put their Post-its onto a flipchart, and then add your own mixed in with theirs.

4. Now give the young person a marker pen or some sticky spots, and ask them to put a spot on the corner of their top three expectations from the total collection, and do this yourself.

5. You should now have a clear list of expectations in order of importance to you both. Discuss with the young person whether these are agreeable.

IN A GROUPWORK SETTING

1. Divide the group into pairs and give each participant a small number of Post-its.

2. Write up on the flipchart 'What I need to work well'.

3. Ask each pair to discuss what they need to work well in the group for two or three minutes.

4. Ask them to write down their needs on Post-its.

5. Ask each young person to place the Post-its onto the flipchart.

6. Give each person three sticky spots and in turns, ask that they put a spot onto the three Post-its that they consider most important for them to work well in the group.

7. Rewrite the expectations in priority order (with the expectation with the most spots at the top) on a new sheet of flipchart paper and display them on the wall, ready to be referred to if they need to be gently re-asserted at any time during the course. If the room is being shared, you will need to take this away and bring it back to display at every session.

Section III:
The Modules

Module 1
Thinking about what I did

Aims of Module 1

- To explore the young person's own feelings, views and values in relation to crime.

- To start to identify your own and the young person's core values.

- To challenge the 'hierarchy of offending' in which young people who offend consider their actions acceptable by comparing them with more serious offending.

- To encourage a wider vocabulary of feelings, looking at the day of the offence and the choices that they made.

- To encourage the young person to think about what they gained and lost from the offence.

- To identify and challenge defensive thinking.

- To explore with the young person what is meant by 'taking responsibility'.

- To encourage the young person to start taking responsibility.

Exercises

Lead-in Exercise 1.1	My opinions, my values.
Lead-in Exercise 1.2	How far would I go?
Lead-in Exercise 1.3	My feelings graph.
Module 1 Core Exercise	Telling it like it was.
Follow-up Exercise 1.1	Excuses, excuses…
Follow-up Exercise 1.2	Am I ready (to take responsibility)?
Follow-up Exercise 1.3	How responsible am I for what happened?
Follow-up Exercise 1.4	Thinking about my crime.

Follow-up Exercise 1.5   Yes I did it, yes it was me.

Follow-up Exercise 1.6   What have I gained, what have I lost?

Follow-up Exercise 1.7   DVD and discussion.

Module 1 Close and evaluation

For groups: Circle Time ideas

AIM

To create consistency and allow the group to relax and get to know each other.

APPROXIMATE TIME

5–10 mins

EQUIPMENT REQUIRED

- Talking piece – e.g. a ball (optional)

SUGGESTED TOPICS

Your name and your favourite food.

Something you are looking forward to.

Share something you have learnt today.

How did you find the experience of the group today?

Remember to start each new session with a review of the previous session.

My opinions, my values

AIMS
To enable the young person to think about their own views in relation to offending. To start the process of identifying values.

APPROXIMATE TIME
10 mins

EQUIPMENT REQUIRED
- scissors
- paper
- masking tape
- marker pen

HANDOUTS NEEDED
My opinions (p.42)

Part 1: My opinions

Instructions
IN A ONE-TO-ONE SETTING

1. Stress that the young person will be asked to think about their own views.

2. Make a line on the floor with masking tape approximately six metres long (the length can be altered to suit the location). Write on a piece of paper TOTALLY AGREE and place it at one end of the line, TOTALLY DISAGREE on another piece and place it at the opposite end of the line, and NOT SURE on a third piece of paper, which should be placed in the middle of the line.

3. Cut up all the statements on the **My opinions** handout on p.42 and give them to the young person.

4. Ask the young person to read out each statement (or read them out yourself if the participant has literacy issues), and then ask them to decide where on the line the statement should be placed. Encourage real honesty in their responses.

IN A GROUPWORK SETTING

1. Repeat steps 1 and 2 from 'In a one-to-one setting' above.

2. Read the first statement from **My opinions** on p.42 out to the group, and ask the participants to stand at the point on the line that corresponds with their opinion about the statement.

3. Without judging their responses generate a debate about each statement, emphasizing honesty and respect for one another's views.

4. Repeat steps 2 and 3 in this section for each statement.

Extension exercise

APPROXIMATE TIME
5 mins

EQUIPMENT REQUIRED
*   marker pen

HANDOUTS NEEDED
none

Make up more statements to fit the participant's particular offence or situation.

Part 2: My values

APPROXIMATE TIME
10 mins

EQUIPMENT REQUIRED
*   newspaper clippings (optional)
*   marker pen

HANDOUTS NEEDED
My values (p.43)
Template 1: Values coin (p.189)

As professionals it is important to be aware of our own core values, and it may also be a helpful exercise to explore values with the participants of this course.

A discussion about values can become complicated, so try to keep it very simple, using everyday examples from people's own experience.

During this exercise and over the rest of the course, pull out any statements, experiences or sentiments expressed by the young person (or group) that expose one of their core values. These might for example relate to:

- a sense of fairness, of justice

- something about trust and trustworthiness

- honesty in actions and/or communication

- integrity and ethical behaviour – doing the right thing

- showing compassion and helping others, particularly those less able to help themselves

- acceptance of diversity, allowing all voices to be heard and every individual to be appreciated

- being respectful of and to one another

- being open-minded, listening to all viewpoints

- the importance of freedom – to be oneself

- being able or willing to do things together, which may include loyalty and commitment to a family, friends, group, team, neighbourhood, country, etc.

- responsibility and being answerable for our actions.

Follow-up Exercise 4.8 on p.178 is a game that considers what would happen if the Martians attacked Planet Earth and imposed their own rules or laws. In the exercise, the Martian laws are carefully written to challenge each of the core values you have gathered during the course. Therefore every time you recognize a value that is expressed or hinted at during an exercise or discussion, reflect it back and check it with the young person or the group. Start up a collection of core values which will continue through the course. You could write the values onto large round gold coloured pieces of card to represent coins or sovereigns, indicating the precious nature of our values (see **Template 1: Values coin** on p.189). The pile of value coins can be added to throughout the course and will form the basis of Follow-up Exercise 4.8 on p.178.

Instructions

IN A ONE-TO-ONE SETTING

1. Give the young person the **My values** handout on p.43.

2. Once they have read the paragraph explaining what values are, strike up a conversation about what values mean to the young person and what their key values are.

IN A GROUPWORK SETTING

1. Give each young person a copy of the **My values** handout on p.43, and ask them to read the statement explaining what values are.

2. Look at the day's news stories and pick a couple of stories where values are highlighted, a teenager who comforts a neighbour whose child has just died, and a footballer who kicks the ball out of play when someone on the other team is injured, for example.

3. This exercise could be turned into a debate, with the young people arguing for one point of view or the other, ending in a general vote among the whole group.

MY OPINIONS

Cut out these statements and decide where they go on the line.

It's fine to lie if it helps you get what you want	Most people who get robbed can afford to lose a few quid
As long as you don't physically injure the person no one is really hurt	Some people deserve to be hit
Offenders should be put in orange overalls when they do community service	Hitting a small child teaches them not to be violent when they grow up
It's okay to walk away from a fight	It's okay to hit someone if they hit you first
People who commit crimes should be punished	Carrying a knife makes you safer
Meeting the person I hurt would make me feel better	Meeting the person I hurt would make them feel better
It is never okay to hit someone	Violence leads to more violence
The people affected by crime are usually to blame	Many people never recover from being a victim of crime
It's the fault of the person I hurt that I'm here	People hurt through crime have a tough time
It's okay to hurt someone in self-defence	Crimes are not crimes if you can get away with them

MY VALUES

Values: Values or beliefs are something that we don't usually think about. However if our values are threatened we certainly know about it! How do we feel when:

- someone pushes in front of us in the queue

- someone hurts a person we love

- our property is taken or damaged.

Those feelings show us that our values are being attacked.

Values are our deepest beliefs that we prize and think are really important. They are about what we value and what is most meaningful in our lives. They are about what we most want for ourselves and others.

Our values are kept so deep inside us that we find it difficult to name them. But they are part of our everyday lives. They guide everything we do and what we decide; our relationships, our friends, our jobs, our entertainment.

LEAD-IN EXERCISE 1.2

How far would I go?

AIMS

To challenge the 'hierarchy of offending' in which young people who offend consider their actions acceptable by comparing them with more serious offending.

To encourage participants to articulate their thinking processes and values.

APPROXIMATE TIME

5–10 mins

EQUIPMENT REQUIRED

- paper
- marker pen

HANDOUTS NEEDED

Template 1: Values coin (p.189)

Instructions

During this exercise and over the rest of the course, pull out any statements, experiences or sentiments expressed by the young person (or group) that expose one of their core values and record them on the values coins (p.189).

IN A ONE-TO-ONE SETTING AND GROUPWORK SETTING

1. Ask the participant(s):

    'Would you take a £10 note that someone left lying around?'

Most people would say yes.

2. Now ask them:

    'What do you feel when you see money on the ground?'

3. Then give them some variables.

    'If you knew it was an elderly person on a pension, would you take it?'

4. Now ask them:

    'What do you feel like if you keep it?'

    'What would you feel if you gave it back to the elderly person?'

5. Now ask:

   'What if it was dropped by a young person in a pub?'

6. and:

   'If you found it on a seat in a cafe where a young woman with a baby had just been?'

7. Try asking:

   'How would you feel if someone came up to you and returned a £10 note that you had just that moment dropped?'

Extension/homework exercise

APPROXIMATE TIME

10–20 mins

EQUIPMENT REQUIRED

- paper
- pens

HANDOUTS NEEDED

This could be the topic for a piece of writing. Pick the statement above that caused the most controversy, or think of a new scenario, and ask the participant(s) to write 100 words about how they would behave in that situation, and why they would behave that way. They could explore:

- What makes it okay to keep money that isn't yours?

- What is it that tells you that it is going too far to keep it?

- What does it feel like to keep money that you know belongs to someone else?

- How would you feel if someone else kept money that they knew was yours?

- How would you feel if someone gave you back money you had dropped or lost?

- How would you feel if you gave someone back some money that they thought they had lost?

LEAD-IN EXERCISE 1.3

My feelings graph

AIM

To encourage a wider vocabulary of feelings and to observe how our emotions change throughout the day, by looking at the day of the offence.

APPROXIMATE TIME

10–15 mins

EQUIPMENT REQUIRED

- coloured paper
- crayons, colouring pencils etc. (optional)
- laser jet address labels (optional)
- masking tape (optional)
- flipchart paper (optional)

HANDOUTS NEEDED

My feelings graph (p.49)
Template 2: Feelings faces (p.190)

A feelings graph is a way of illustrating how our feelings change throughout the day. Many people who commit crimes are able to identify an experience or circumstance leading up to the offence that made them unhappy, often involving some kind of loss.

You may like to have a supply of art resources available, including coloured paper, stickers of smiley and sad faces, crayons, etc. to help the young person engage with the exercise. The cartoon faces on **Template 2: Feelings faces** on p.190 can be cut up and glued or placed onto the graph. It is also possible to buy laser jet address labels that are A4-sized to turn the page into stickers.

Instructions
IN A ONE-TO-ONE SETTING AND GROUP SETTING

1. Give each participant a copy of the **My feelings graph** handout on p.49, and keep a copy for yourself.

2. Explain that the vertical axis represents how the young person felt, with very unhappy at the bottom and very happy at the top, and the horizontal axis represents the time, from waking to bedtime.

3. Demonstrate to the young person how to fill in the graph. In drawing your own example graph, show how events during the day lead to peaks and troughs of feelings and emotions. Point out if you think there is a default position somewhere in the middle.

4. Ask the participant(s) to draw a feelings graph for the day on which they committed the offence that led to them being on this course (or for one of the offences if there were several). If the young person needs to practise the technique, you could ask them to choose any day they like to do a feelings graph for, as a lead-in to this exercise. Make sure you have plenty of extra handouts.

5. Ask the young person to annotate the graph with the thoughts they had at different points of the day, to help establish the link between thoughts and feelings.

6. The graph can be adapted to cover the week of the offence, if significant events would otherwise be missed. Simply ask the young person to draw the graph on a sheet of flipchart paper, with each day listed on the horizontal axis.

7. Discuss how they found the exercise and whether it produced any surprises. In a groupwork setting the young people could share their graphs in pairs and then with the whole group.

Alternative exercise

The graph could be turned into a more active exercise with the axes laid out on the floor using masking tape. The participant(s) should stand on the line in the position appropriate to their feeling at a given time. You could ask the participant(s):

'How did you feel when you first woke up?'

'What about by mid-afternoon?'

'When you were having your dinner, how did you feel then?'

You could also try asking them at what point in the day they felt most sad, and at what point they felt most happy.

Extension exercise

APPROXIMATE TIME

5–10 mins

EQUIPMENT REQUIRED

- flipchart paper
- pen

HANDOUTS NEEDED

A feelings graph can be drawn on a sheet of flipchart paper for the young person's life from birth to the present day. Having introduced the feelings graph early in the course, this exercise is used in later exercises to represent the different people who were affected by the young person's crime.

MY FEELINGS GRAPH

The two lines make a graph. Along the bottom line is the time from when you woke up to when you went to bed. The vertical line is from very sad at the bottom to very happy at the top. Draw a line to show your feelings and how they went up and down during that day. You could write what was happening next to the line.

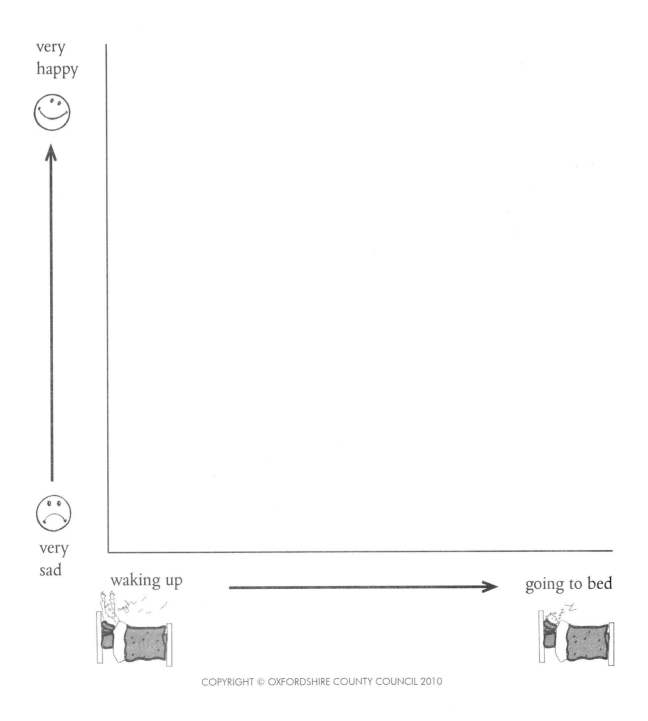

very
happy

very
sad

waking up   going to bed

MODULE I CORE EXERCISE
Telling it like it was

AIMS

To encourage and effect change in the young person, towards taking responsibility and feeling accountable for their actions.

By telling their story again new possibilities for acceptance, movement and change may open up, which can be transformative. Revisiting what happened with the young person, we can look for signs of change, helping them to see the experience in a new light.

Part I: Thoughts and feelings

APPROXIMATE TIME

10–30 mins

EQUIPMENT REQUIRED

- flipchart paper/white board
- marker pens/coloured pens and pencils
- objects to symbolize people or property (optional)
- video/smart board (optional)
- laser jet address labels (optional)

HANDOUTS NEEDED

Template 3: Thought and feelings bubbles (p.191)

This exercise involves the participant drawing a timeline like the one shown in Figure 1 on p.51, leading from the time before the incident leading to the young person being on this course, to the incident itself, and then to the time after the incident. The explosion shape indicates the incident. The young person is encouraged to tell their own story of the events leading up to, during and after the incident. They should identify their thoughts and feelings at each key point up and down the timeline, by writing in the thought and feelings bubbles. Be prepared to expand the timeline, for example to include 'before' as well as 'just before', or 'now' as well as 'just after' to capture significant events.

Although the 'telling the story' part of the exercise can be done verbally or in writing, it could equally be done as pictures or cartoons, using video, a smart board or through role play.

Keep the timeline fluid and expandable, so that the young person can come up with other key stages or incidents that they feel are of relevance to the crime.

It will be interesting to explore with the young person whether what they say, think and feel were all in sync on the day of the incident. We can all remember times when we have suppressed feelings, for example fear or panic, and continued to do something despite those inner warnings. Or sometimes we have ignored a voice in our head telling us that what we are doing is wrong. It may be, for example, that peer pressure leads young people into actions that their best instincts are telling them to avoid.

Instructions
IN A ONE-TO-ONE SETTING

1. Ask the young person to draw a timeline on flipchart paper or a white board. You may like to do an example one yourself first to show them.

2. Cut out **Template 3: Thought and feelings bubbles** on p.191 to give to the young person to write on and attach at appropriate points in the

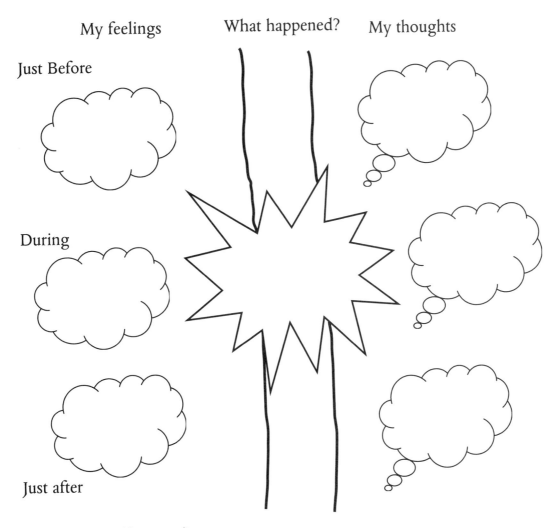

Figure 1 Telling it like it was diagram

story. It is possible to buy laser jet address labels that are A4-sized to turn the templates into stickers.

IN A GROUPWORK SETTING

1. Ask the participants to draw the timeline on flipchart paper or a white board. You may like to do an example one yourself first to show them.

2. Cut out **Template 3: Thought and feelings bubbles** on p.191 to give to the participants to write on and attach at appropriate points in the story. It is possible to buy laser jet address labels that are A4-sized to turn the templates into stickers.

3. The young people can work on their story individually or in pairs, and then share them in front of the group, answering questions from the participants for clarity. Encourage respectful listening.

Extension exercise 1

APPROXIMATE TIME
10–20 mins

EQUIPMENT REQUIRED
- flipchart paper
- marker pens

HANDOUTS NEEDED
Template 3: Thought and feelings bubbles (p.191)

Repeat the exercise, considering what other people might have thought and felt at each stage, exploring the fact that different people affected by the incident all have their own stories to tell.

Extension exercise 2

APPROXIMATE TIME
1 hour–1 day

EQUIPMENT REQUIRED
- transport to scene of the incident
- camera
- access to internet mapping programme

HANDOUTS NEEDED
none

The young person's story of the incident can be drawn out in many creative ways. In some cases it can be powerful to revisit the crime scene. Photos could be taken, or the young person could narrate a video recording, replaying the events on camera. The events on that day could be mapped using an internet mapping programme. These techniques can be particularly helpful if the young person is finding it difficult to be clear about events.

Part 2: My choices
APPROXIMATE TIME
10–15 mins

EQUIPMENT REQUIRED
- flipchart paper
- marker pens/coloured pens and pencils
- objects to symbolize people or property (optional)

HANDOUTS NEEDED
Telling it like it was Part 2 (p.57)
Template 1: Values coin (p.189)
Template 3: Thought and feelings bubbles (p.191)

Figure 2: Explosion shape

The circumstances that lead to a crime may be complex, and often involve some factors or events within the young person's control, about which they will have made choices, and other factors or events that were not within their control. The young person needs to take responsibility for their own choices, and it can be helpful to map out all the other factors involved, so that they can own the area they should take responsibility for. If this isn't made clear they may be tempted to push the blame onto the other people or circumstances and minimize their own part in the crime.

Values

During this exercise and over the rest of the course, pull out any statements, experiences or sentiments expressed by the young person (or group) that expose one of their core values and record them on the values coins (p.189).

Instructions
IN A ONE-TO-ONE SETTING

1. Identify through discussion with the young person any significant factors leading up to the incident.

2. Give the young person a sheet of flipchart paper, and ask them to draw the explosion shape in Figure 2 on p.53, with several large circles around the outside.

3. Ask the young person to write or draw images in the circles to signify the factors that led up to the incident, for example using stick people for others involved. You could alternatively use objects or symbols to place on the picture. If they are struggling with this exercise, give the young person a copy of the **Telling it like it was Part 2** handout on p.57 now.

4. To explore how important each factor was in causing the incident, ask the participant to rate them, from 5 for very important to 1 for unimportant, or colour code them, by using a dark colour for the most important and light colour for least important, for example. They could also use different colours to explore how each of the factors they have identified makes them feel (Module 2 Lead-in Exercise 2.1: Me as a victim on p.94–5 contains notes on colours and emotions).

5. Referring to the completed exercise, ask the participant to look again at the range of factors on the handout, and identify which of them involved choices that they themselves made, that led to the incident occurring. If they did not need the **Telling it like it was Part 2** handout on p.57 earlier, give them this now.

6. You could say:

'These are the parts of the incident that you are responsible for'

Repeat this by exploring other choices that they might have made, or that they could make if similar circumstances were to arise. Stress that everyone makes mistakes, and what is important is that they learn from this one.

7. Ask:

'If you keep out of trouble, who would be most surprised?'

'If you keep out of trouble, who will be most pleased?'

IN A GROUPWORK SETTING

1. Identify through discussion with the young people any significant factors leading up to the incident.

2. Give the participants a sheet of flipchart paper each, and ask them to draw the explosion shape above, with several large circles around the outside. They should work individually on this part of the exercise.

3. Ask the young person to write or draw images to signify the factors that led up to the incident, for example using stick people for others involved. You could alternatively offer them a variety of objects to place on the picture. If any of the group are struggling with this exercise, give them a copy of the **Telling it like it was Part 2** handout on p.57 at this point.

4. To explore how important each factor was in causing the incident, ask the participant to rate them, from 5 for very important to 1 for unimportant, or colour code them by using a dark colour for the most important and light colour for the least important, for example. They could also use different colours to explore how each of the factors they have identified makes them feel (Module 2 Lead-in Exercise 2.1: Me as a victim on p.94–5 contains notes on colours and emotions).

5. Referring to the completed exercise, ask the participants to look again at the range of factors on the handout, and identify which of them involved choices that they themselves made, that led to the incident occurring. If any of the participants did not need the **Telling it like it was Part 2** handout on p.57 earlier, give them this now. They can write down their answers on the handout or just think about them if they prefer.

6. Going round the group, ask each participant to say which factors from their picture they feel they are responsible for. Then ask the rest of the group if they agree.

7. Repeat this by exploring other choices that they might have made, or that they could make if similar circumstances were to arise. Stress that everyone makes mistakes, and what is important is that they learn from this one.

8. Going round the group, ask each participant:

'If you keep out of trouble, who would be most surprised?'

'If you keep out of trouble, who will be most pleased?'

Extension exercise

APPROXIMATE TIME
10–20 mins

EQUIPMENT REQUIRED

- flipchart paper
- news cuttings/videos (optional)

HANDOUTS NEEDED
Telling it like it was Part 2 (p.57)

This exercise can also be done using made-up scenarios, news cuttings or videos, etc. to explore different offences and different factors which can play a part in crime.

Looking to the future

During this exercise the young person may be able to clarify the factors surrounding the incident, and how their choices led them into trouble. They may show a commitment to making better choices should similar circumstances occur. However some of the behaviours leading to the incident (for example misuse of drugs or alcohol, hanging round with pro-criminal peers, living in a deprived neighbourhood) may be difficult to change, and some factors (e.g. lack of support at home or poor attitudes from parents) may continue regardless of changes in the young person.

What will happen if the young person finds themselves back in the same circumstances? What if they are feeling the same negative feelings that they identify in the lead up to their crime?

This may be a point in the course where it is important to draw in wider support for the young person to address these wider offence-related needs, or to link the victim empathy work in with other interventions that may be available, which could include parenting support, substance misuse work, offending behaviour work, mentoring, reparation, positive activities, etc. Try to avoid a situation where needs are identified and the commitment to change is articulated, without the appropriate support to maintain that change.

TELLING IT LIKE IT WAS
PART 2

Read the list of factors that could have influenced what happened below.

The range of different factors that might have been involved could include:

- The presence of others (e.g. I was showing off in front of my mates)

- The action of others (e.g. they hit me first)

- Feelings (e.g. Things have been bad since my parents divorced)

- Disinhibitors (e.g. I was drunk)

- Chance factors (e.g. I found that the car window was open)

- Internal factors (e.g. I get angry really quickly)

- Social factors (e.g. There is nothing to do round here)

- Environmental factors (e.g. the place was a mess before I arrived)

- Practical matters (e.g. I was skint)

Which ones did you have a choice about?

What other choices could you have made?

FOLLOW-UP EXERCISE 1.1

Excuses, excuses...

AIM
To identify and challenge defensive thinking.

APPROXIMATE TIME
10–15 mins

EQUIPMENT REQUIRED
- flipchart paper
- pens
- marker pens
- scissors for cutting out the statements on the handout **Excuses, excuses... (2)**. You should judge for yourself whether to cut out the statements for the participants yourself, or hand out scissors to the young people.
- card/paper

HANDOUTS NEEDED
Defensive thinking (p.62)
Excuses, excuses... (1) (p.63)
Excuses, excuses... (2) (p.64)

Start by explaining to the young person that we all say things to ourselves to make us feel good about ourselves. This is an important thing to do in terms of building self-esteem and confidence. Denial is essentially a healthy and okay stage for people who may not yet be ready, or may be too shocked to look at their offence. However, they will need to move on from it. What we say to ourselves can become a way of justifying, excusing or rationalizing negative behaviour.

This can sometimes be referred to as *defensive thinking* – making excuses or refusing to take full responsibility for what we do in order to feel better about ourselves. For example, if someone says that they are not a smoker, but they smoke socially when they go out – then they are not admitting to themselves or others that they are a smoker (which they obviously are!). Or, someone who says that they haven't got an alcohol problem as they don't need a drink every day, but who drinks vast amounts at the weekend and often ends up in fights, is not admitting that their alcohol use is problematic. This form of defence statement is denial.

There are five main types of defensive thinking that this course addresses, set out in the table on the **Defensive thinking** handout on p.62.

Instructions
IN A ONE-TO-ONE SETTING

1. You could try saying something like:

   'Many people who commit crimes make excuses for their behaviour following an arrest. They blame other people or pressures for their involvement with the crime.'

2. You could ask:

   'Why do people use defensive thinking?'

3. You could ask:

   'What types of excuse can you think of?'

4. Instigate a discussion about general offending behaviour, asking for examples of different types of offences and the types of justifications that may be used, to help clarify understanding. If they struggle with this, help the young person out by suggesting different types of offences and even some of the statements you have heard in your own experience, asking them what form of distortion the example is. Try to elicit excuses first, and be prepared to be flexible with the exercise if different excuses are suggested from the ones below.

5. Give the participant a copy of the **Defensive thinking** handout on p.62 and discuss other day-to-day examples that they can think of (especially thinking of people they know) for each type. Encourage each participant to think of at least one new offence, strategy and defence each and fill it in on the handout.

6. You could ask:

   'What if your offence had been committed by someone else against a member of your family? How would you feel about that?'

7. If their responses are vague, be sure to reflect back any inconsistencies that they make or gaps in statements and clarify what they mean.

8. Give each participant a copy of the **Excuses, excuses… (1)** (p.63) and **Excuses, excuses… (2)** (p.64) handouts, and a pair of scissors.

9. Ask the young person to cut out the statements on the handout **Excuses, excuses… (2)**. Alternatively, you could ask the young person to make some

cards themselves, featuring pictures or cartoons to symbolize defensive thinking, such as 'The Minimizer', 'The Denier', etc.

10. They then have to place the cards on the correct square for the appropriate defensive thinking category.

11. You could initiate a discussion about whether the criminal justice system encourages defensive thinking (e.g. defence solicitors, separating the parties involved in an incident, punishing the perpetrator, etc.).

IN A GROUPWORK SETTING

1. You could try saying something like:

   'Many people who commit crimes make excuses for their behaviour following an arrest. They blame other people or pressures for their involvement with the crime.'

2. You could ask:

   'Why do people use defensive thinking?'

3. You could ask:

   'What types of excuse can you think of?'

4. Instigate a discussion about general offending behaviour, asking for examples of different types of offences and the types of justifications that may be used, to help clarify understanding. If they struggle with this, help the young person out by suggesting different types of offences and even some of the statements you have heard in your own experience, asking them what form of distortion the example is. Try to elicit excuses first, and be prepared to be flexible with the exercise if different excuses are suggested to the ones below.

5. Give each participant a copy of the **Defensive thinking** handout on p.62 and discuss other day-to-day examples that they can think of (especially thinking of people they know) for each type. Encourage each participant to think of at least one new offence, strategy and defence each and fill it in on the handout.

6. You could ask:

   'What if your offence had been committed by someone else against a member of your family? How would you feel about that?'

7. If their responses are vague, be sure to reflect back any inconsistencies that they make or gaps in statements and clarify what they mean.

8.   Write down the defensive thinking categories from **Excuses, excuses… (1)** on a sheet of flipchart paper. Cut out the statement cards on the **Excuses, excuses… (2)** handout and give them out to the participants.

9.   The participants take it in turns to read out a card from the pile and place it in the appropriate square. They may put it on a line if they think it could belong to more than one category. Accept their answers and draw out the thinking behind their choice rather than correcting them. After each participant has put their card on their chosen square, you should check this with the rest of the group.

Extension exercise

APPROXIMATE TIME

5 mins

EQUIPMENT REQUIRED

HANDOUTS NEEDED

Look back over the Module 1 Core Exercise ('Telling it like it was', p.50). Discuss with the participant(s) whether there has been any evidence of defensive thinking in their thoughts or statements.

✓

DEFENSIVE THINKING

We all want to feel good about ourselves. Sometimes we do something we know is wrong. We don't want to feel bad inside, so we make excuses. This is called defensive thinking.

Offence	Strategies people use to make themselves feel OK about it	Defence
e.g. House burglary	'They were insured anyway. It won't cost them anything'	Minimization
e.g. Section 18 GBH	'They fell on to my knife – I didn't stab them'	Denial
e.g. Assault	'She was winding me up'	Victim blaming
e.g. Criminal damage	'I was drunk. I didn't know what I was doing'	Denial of self-control
e.g. Shop theft	'I needed it so I took it'	Entitlement
e.g.		

EXCUSES, EXCUSES... (1)

Work out which square each statement on **Excuses, excuses... (2)** belongs in.

Making it seem smaller (*minimization*)	Saying it was the other person's fault (*victim blaming*)
Thinking you are owed things without earning them (*entitlement*)	
Saying it wasn't you (*denial*)	Saying you couldn't help it (*denial of self-control*)

EXCUSES, EXCUSES... (2)

'I only did it because everyone else was doing it'

'They were insured anyway. It won't cost them anything'

'I blacked out'

'I only hit him once'

'They fell on to my knife – I didn't stab them'

'I can't remember what happened'

'She was winding me up'

'I was drunk. I didn't know what I was doing'

'He shouldn't have looked at me that way'

'They started it'

'It didn't really hurt them'

'I was there but I didn't do anything'

'When I'm angry I lose control and don't know what I'm doing'

'It was everyone else who did it'

'They just fell over – I didn't even push them'

'They've got another car – who needs more than one?'

'Everyone has one – why shouldn't I?'

'No one cares – it's no big deal'

Am I ready (to take responsibility)?

AIMS

To explore the meanings of the word 'responsibility', and start to challenge the young person about their own areas of responsibility.

To see how our choices lead to responsibility, and how we are responsible for the choices we make.

Part 1: The word 'responsibility'

APPROXIMATE TIME

5–10 mins

EQUIPMENT REQUIRED

- pens

HANDOUTS NEEDED

Part 1: The word 'responsibility' (p.68)

Instructions

IN A ONE-TO-ONE SETTING

1. Explain that this section of the course is looking at the meaning of the word 'responsibility'.

2. Ask the young person to read the sentences on the handout **Part 1: The word 'responsibility'** on p.68. Ask them if they can think of another word (or words) to replace the words in italics in each of the sentences. They can write this on the line below, or just say it.

3. Ask the young person to think of other sentences with the word *responsible* or *responsibility* in them.

4. Have a discussion about what the word 'responsibility' means. You could ask:

    'Has anyone ever said it to you?'

    'Where were you and what were you doing?'

IN A GROUP WORK SETTING

1. Explain that this section of the course is looking at the meaning of the word 'responsibility'.

2. Ask the participants to read the sentences on the handout **Part 1: The word 'responsibility'** on p.68. Ask them if they can think of another word (or words) to replace the words in italics in each of the sentences. They can write this on the line below, or just say it.

3. Ask the participants to think of other sentences with the word *responsible* or *responsibility* in them.

4. Have a discussion about what the word 'responsibility' means. You could ask:

   'Has anyone ever said it to you?'

   'In what context?'

Part 2: Three meanings for 'responsibility'

APPROXIMATE TIME
5–10 mins

EQUIPMENT REQUIRED

- pens
- flipchart paper (group)
- scissors (optional)

HANDOUTS NEEDED
Part 2: Three meanings for 'responsibility' (1) (p.69)
Part 2: Three meanings for 'responsibility' (2) (p.70)

Discuss the different meanings for 'responsibility', which fall into three categories:

- **Accepting I did it** (implying blame, liability and accountability).

- **Accepting I need to sort it out** (talking about a conflict or task).

- **Accepting I won't do it again** (describing dependability, reliability and trustworthiness).

Instructions
IN A ONE-TO-ONE SETTING

Ask the young person to fit the statements from the handout **Part 2: Three meanings for 'responsibility' (2)** on p.70 into the three categories on **Part 2: Three meanings for 'responsibility' (1)** on p.69.

IN A GROUPWORK SETTING

1. Write down the three meanings for responsibility from the handout **Part 2: Three meanings for 'responsibility' (1)** on a sheet of flipchart paper. Cut out the statement cards from **Part 2: Three meanings for 'responsibility' (2)** and give them out to the participants.

2. The participants take it in turns to read out a card and place it in the appropriate square. They may put it on a line if they think it could belong to more than one category. Accept their answers and draw out the thinking behind their choice rather than correcting them. After each participant has put their card on their chosen square, you should check this with the rest of the group.

Part 3: Am I ready?
APPROXIMATE TIME
5 mins

EQUIPMENT REQUIRED
- pens

HANDOUTS NEEDED
Part 3: Am I ready? (p.71)

In hoping that the young person will take responsibility, we are hoping that they will: accept their part in what happened (past); accept their duty to do something about it (present); and become more trustworthy and reliable (future).

Instructions
IN A ONE-TO-ONE OR GROUPWORK SETTING

Ask the young person to consider whether they are ready to take responsibility in accepting their part in what happened (past), their duty to do something about it (present) and in becoming more trustworthy and reliable (future), by writing 'yes,' 'no' or 'maybe' (or anything else they choose) in the relevant circles on the handout **Part 3: Am I ready?** on p.71.

PART 1: THE WORD 'RESPONSIBILITY'

Read the sentences. See if you can think of another way of saying the bit in italic so that it means the same. Write your way on the line.

Ryan wasn't convicted for the burglary because he is *below the age of criminal responsibility*

_____

Police are trying to find the *person responsible for* the arson attack

_____

Sahib was a good dad because *he took responsibility for* bringing up his son

_____

Jasmin saw the stabbing but didn't do anything, and when she heard they'd died *she felt responsible*

_____

PART 2: THREE MEANINGS FOR 'RESPONSIBILITY' (1)

Place the sentences onto the correct definition of 'responsibility'

Accepting
I did it

Accepting I need
to sort it out

Accepting I won't
do it again

PART 2: THREE MEANINGS FOR 'RESPONSIBILITY' (2)

'I will try to be more responsible in the future'

'I better sort it out since it was my mess'

'I am responsible for what I did'

'I will be responsible for putting it right'

'It definitely won't happen again'

'I admit it – it was me'

PART 3: AM I READY?

Write 'Yes', 'No' or 'Maybe' in the three circles.

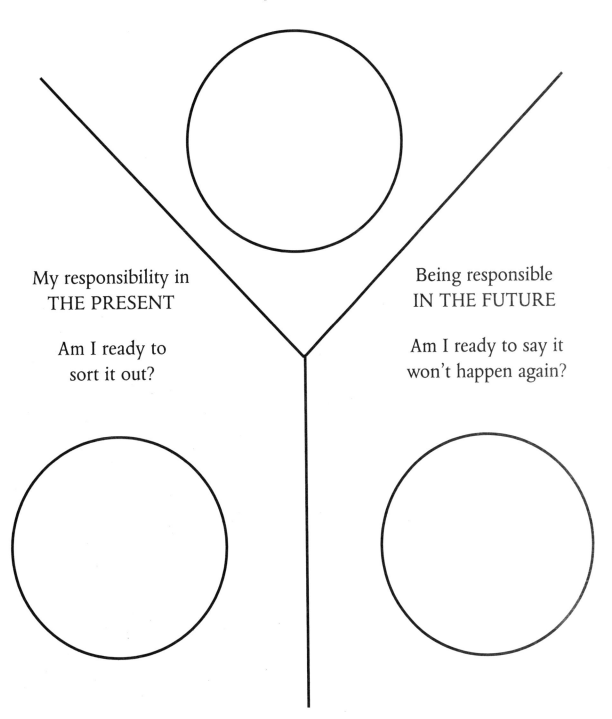

Taking responsibility for THE PAST
Am I ready to accept what I did?

My responsibility in
THE PRESENT

Am I ready to
sort it out?

Being responsible
IN THE FUTURE

Am I ready to say it
won't happen again?

How responsible am I for what happened?

AIM

To map out the young person's area of responsibility for what happened and to identify what other factors were involved.

Part 1

APPROXIMATE TIME
10–15 mins

EQUIPMENT REQUIRED

- masking tape
- flipchart paper
- marker pen

HANDOUTS NEEDED
none

Instructions

IN A ONE-TO-ONE SETTING

1. Make a line on the floor with masking tape. Write on a piece of paper 0% (not at all responsible) and place it at one end of the line and 100% (fully responsible) on another piece and place it at the opposite end of the line.

2. Use the scenarios below as examples, and to provoke discussion. Read out the first part of the scenario, and ask the participant to stand on the line of responsibility where they would place the person who offended.

3. Then read out the mitigating/aggravating factor of the scenario, and ask whether they would like to change their mind and move to a different place along the line.

4. Then ask the question at the bottom of each example, e.g. *'Where would the relatives of the family who were killed place his responsibility?'*

5. Responsibility may be shared, for example by co-defendants or circumstances that led to the incident. These factors can be added to the floor diagram. For example, you could make a second line to indicate

the responsibility that another person shares for the incident and stand on that line yourself, or draw pictures to signify circumstances, such as peer pressure, and place these on the line. You could suggest that the participant thinks of the other factors or people.

IN A GROUPWORK SETTING

1. Make a line on the floor with masking tape approximately three to ten metres long depending on the size of the room. Write on a piece of paper 0% (not at all responsible) and place it at one end of the line and 100% (fully responsible) on another piece and place it at the opposite end of the line.

2. Use the scenarios below as examples, and to provoke discussion. Read out the first part of the scenario, and ask one of the participants to volunteer to stand on the line of responsibility where they would place the person who offended. Ask the rest of the group if they agree.

3. Then read out the mitigating/aggravating factor of the scenario, and ask the group if they would like to change their mind and move the volunteer to a different place along the line.

4. Then ask the question at the bottom of each example, e.g. *'Where would the relatives place his responsibility?'*

5. Responsibility may be shared, for example by co-defendants or circumstances that led to the incident. These factors can be added to the visual diagram. For example, you could make a second line to indicate the responsibility that another person shares for the incident and ask another participant to stand on that line. Other members of the group could signify circumstances, such as peer pressure, and be placed on the line. You could suggest that the participants think of the other factors or people.

Scenarios

1. A driver, twice over the limit, kills a family of four in a head on collision. Add a *mitigating factor*, re: shared responsibility with others:

> *What if the driver didn't want to drive but was persuaded to by his/her mates who wanted a lift home?*

Ask:

> *'Where would the relatives of the family who were killed place his responsibility?'*

2.   A girl stamps on another girl's head.

Add a *mitigating factor* re: provocation from the victim.

> *What if it happened after an insult about her mum (who was disabled)*

Ask:

> *'Where would the girl who committed the offence place her own responsibility?'*

3.   A 15-year-old is found in possession of a hunting knife at school.

Add a *mitigating factor* re: availability of the weapon.

> *What if it was bought at a shop in the High Street?*

Ask:

> *'Where would the magistrates place his responsibility?'*

4.   A boy pushes over another boy during a fight.

Add an *aggravating factor* re: consequences for the victim.

> *What if the victim ends up with permanent brain injury after his head hits the pavement?*

Ask:

> *'Where would the victim's parent or carer place his responsibility?'*

Part 2

APPROXIMATE TIME
5–10 mins

EQUIPMENT REQUIRED
- masking tape
- objects (such as coins and pebbles)

HANDOUTS NEEDED
none

Instructions
IN A ONE-TO-ONE SETTING

1.   After using the scenarios above (you may like to choose examples of your own to suit the individual), turn to the young person's own actions that led to them being placed on this course.

2.   Ask them to place themselves at the point along the line that indicates how responsible they feel personally for what happened. As with the

scenarios, discuss whether other people share any of the responsibility, and whether there were other factors that led to the offence. These can be placed on the floor diagram as above in Part 1.

3. After identifying all the other people involved and other factors that led to the incident, isolate again the young person's own responsibility. Ask them:

    'How responsible are you for your part of what happened?'

Ask:

'Where might the people who were hurt by your actions place you on the line of responsibility?'

Ask:

'What did the Crown Prosecution Service (CPS) say about your responsibility?'

4. As with the scenarios, you could stretch the point to consider, for example, whether the young person would move themselves along the responsibility scale if, say, someone had died, if it turned out to be a friend whose property they stole or damaged, if they hadn't been caught, etc.

IN A GROUPWORK SETTING

1. After using the scenarios above (you may like to choose examples of your own to suit the individuals in the group), turn to the young persons' own actions.

2. Ask each participant to place themselves at the point along the line that indicates how responsible they feel personally for what happened. As with the scenarios, discuss whether other people share any of the responsibility, and whether there were other factors that led to the incident. These can be added to the floor diagram by drawing pictures, or using objects to signify the other people or circumstances.

3. After identifying all the other people involved and other factors that led to the incident, isolate again the young person's own responsibility. Ask them:

    'How responsible are you for your part of what happened?'

Ask:

'Where might the people who were hurt by your actions place you on the line of responsibility?'

Ask:

'What did the CPS say about your responsibility?'

4.   As with the scenarios, you could stretch the point to consider, for example, whether the young person would move themselves along the responsibility scale if, say, someone had died, if it turned out to be a friend whose property they stole or damaged, if they hadn't been caught, etc.

Thinking about my crime

AIMS

To explore and map out with the young person their feelings about their actions, identifying key issues such as responsibility, accountability and remorse.
To encourage honesty, reflection and discussion.

APPROXIMATE TIME

5–10 mins

EQUIPMENT REQUIRED

- coloured pens or pencils
- lined paper

HANDOUTS NEEDED

Thinking about my crime (p.79)

This exercise could be used as an assessment tool to establish the young person's attitude and the degree to which they are taking responsibility.

During this exercise, remain neutral and non-judgemental (but curious) about the young person's responses. Use it as a discussion opener, to help them to explore their own thoughts, attitudes and values. Allow them to keep their own sense of dignity.

Instructions
IN A ONE-TO-ONE AND GROUPWORK SETTING

1. Ask the participant(s) to colour in each circle in the diagram either green for 'that's what I think', yellow for 'that's partly what I think' or red for 'I don't think that at all'. Take time to discuss their choices.

2. When they have finished, you could ask them to construct a long sentence (or paragraph) on a piece of paper to sum up their responses, e.g.
    'I was there and I did part of it, and although I meant to do it I shouldn't have done it and I do care a bit about it… etc.'

3. Check whether this sounds correct to the young person.

Extension exercise

APPROXIMATE TIME

5–10 mins

EQUIPMENT REQUIRED

- pens

HANDOUTS NEEDED

What other people might think about my crime (p.80)

Instructions

IN A ONE-TO-ONE SETTING

1. Go round the circle on the **Thinking about my crime** handout again and explore if there would be any differences in responses in different circumstances and from different points of view, for example what the young person's solicitor advised them to say. You can choose to simply discuss this, or ask the young person to write down their thoughts on the **What other people might think about my crime** handout.

2. Keep the participant's coloured in sheet and revisit it later on in the course to see if there are any changes.

IN A GROUPWORK SETTING

1. Go round the circle on the **Thinking about my crime** handout again and explore if there would be any differences in responses in different circumstances and from different points of view, for example what the young person's solicitor advised them to say. The young people could work on their answers alone or in pairs, and then share and discuss them with the group as a whole.

2. You can choose to simply discuss this, or ask the participants to write down their thoughts on the **What other people might think about my crime** handout.

3. Keep the participants' coloured in sheets and revisit them later on in the course to see if there are any changes.

THINKING ABOUT MY CRIME

Think about your crime. Look at each circle. Colour each one in:

GREEN = that's what I think

YELLOW = that's partly what I think

RED = I don't think that at all

I would do the same again

I was there

I did it

I'm glad I was caught

I meant to do it

I tell others about it

I did it for a good reason

I am sorry about it

I shouldn't have done it

It was wrong

I care about it

✓

WHAT OTHER PEOPLE MIGHT THINK ABOUT MY CRIME

- What you thought immediately afterwards

_____

_____

- What the court (or police) will think about your crime

_____

_____

- What your solicitor advised you to say

_____

_____

- What the person you hurt might say

_____

_____

- What your friends think

_____

_____

FOLLOW-UP EXERCISE 1.5

Yes I did it, yes it was me

AIMS

To explore what feelings accompany taking responsibility for our mistakes.
To encourage emotional literacy.

Part 1

APPROXIMATE TIME

5–20 mins

EQUIPMENT REQUIRED

- coloured pens or crayons

HANDOUTS NEEDED

Yes I did it, yes it was me, Part 1 (p.85)

This exercise seeks to identify the feelings that we have when taking responsibility for our mistakes. Refer to and remind participants of any previous exercises they have completed that concern responsibility.

Instructions
IN A ONE-TO-ONE SETTING

1. On the **Yes I did it, yes it was me, Part 1** handout, ask the young person to circle any feelings they have when they are considering their area of responsibility for the incident that led to them being placed on the course.

2. Ask them to add expressions and colours to the mask to represent most closely the emotions identified. If some time has passed since the incident, there may not be strong emotions, and some young people may have difficulty identifying their feelings. If this is the case, offer gentle encouragement.

3. Ask the young person:

    'Did it feel different straight after the incident?'

    'If so, what has made your feelings change?'

    'Think about the reaction of your parent/carer when you say, "Yes I did it, yes it was me..." Are there any different feelings now?'

4. Take care to monitor the responses to this exercise, and to provide follow-up support if a young person is indicating a high level of distress. Refer to 'Notes for facilitators' on p.15.

IN A GROUPWORK SETTING

1. On the **Yes I did it, yes it was me, Part 1** handout, ask the participants to circle any feelings they have when they think about their area of responsibility for the incident.

2. Ask them to add expressions and colours to the mask to represent most closely the emotions identified. If some time has passed since the incident, there may not be strong emotions, and some young people may have difficulty identifying their feelings. If this is the case, offer gentle encouragement.

3. Ask the young person:

   'Did it feel different straight after the incident?'

   'If so, what has made your feelings change?'

   'Think about the reaction of your parent/carer when you say "Yes I did it, yes it was me…" Are there any different feelings now?'

4. Take care to monitor the responses to this exercise, and to provide follow-up support if a young person is indicating a high level of distress. Refer to 'Notes for facilitators' on p.15.

Extension/homework exercise

APPROXIMATE TIME

20 mins–2 hours

EQUIPMENT REQUIRED

- card
- coloured pens or crayons

HANDOUTS NEEDED

You could ask the young person to make their mask, either with papier-maché, or on a piece of card. This could be turned into a piece of artwork. If you choose to do this in the session, you will need to allow at least 20 minutes for this exercise, you might consider setting this as a piece of homework.

Part 2

APPROXIMATE TIME

5–15 minutes

EQUIPMENT REQUIRED

* pens

HANDOUTS NEEDED

Yes I did it, Yes it was me, Part 2 (p.86)

The exercise in Part 1 above aims to lead the young person or group towards a better understanding of responsibility and what it means for them. Those who are less responsive, who may have been (or remain) on the receiving end of bad parenting and lack of positive role models may be left feeling, 'So what? What's in it for me?' It can be scary and daunting to know that you have choices, and perversely comforting to remain a victim.

The answer, it is hoped, is that in taking responsibility they will start to feel more empowered and sense the positive emotions that flow from it. These may include feeling more in control, improved self-esteem and, if the support is there, a future path of positive reinforcement.

To sow the seed, this exercise attempts to identify whether the young person can sense this more positive future for themselves. It may be appropriate to include one of the Follow-up exercises from Module 4 at this point to further reinforce those feelings; we recommend Follow-up Exercise 4.5 (My harmony tree) on p.167, Follow-up Exercise 4.6 (What makes a good role model?) on p.170, Follow-up Exercise 4.7 (What others think of me) on p.173 or Follow-up Exercise 4.9 (Looking to the future) on p.180.

In this exercise the young person chooses on a scale between two opposite feelings words when asked:

> *'Thinking **I have choices** makes me feel…'*

and

> *'Thinking **I take responsibility** makes me feel…'*

By joining the crosses into a line the young person can gauge whether their current feelings are positive or negative overall.

Instructions
IN A ONE-TO-ONE AND GROUPWORK SETTING

1. Give each young person two copies each of **Yes I did it, yes it was me, Part 2** on p.85.

2. Ask them to answer the question below honestly and put an X in the place along the line that most reflects their feelings:

    *'Thinking **I have choices** makes me feel…'*

3. Now ask them to answer the next question on a new handout:

    *'Thinking **I take responsibility** makes me feel…'*

4. Now ask them to join up the crosses, and ask them how they feel.

YES I DID IT, YES IT WAS ME, PART 1

Think about your responsibility for what happened. Circle the feelings that thinking about it makes you feel. Where there are lines, feel free to add your own words.

Draw on the mask with an expression and colours for those feelings.

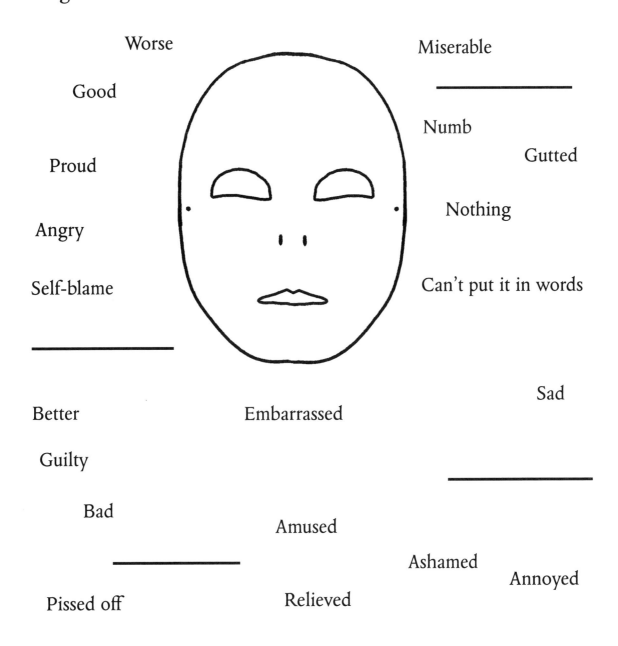

Worse

Miserable

Good

_____

Numb

Proud

Gutted

Angry

Nothing

Self-blame

Can't put it in words

_____

Sad

Better

Embarrassed

Guilty

_____

Bad

Amused

_____

Ashamed

Annoyed

Pissed off

Relieved

YES I DID IT, YES IT WAS ME, PART 2

Put an X on the line for how each sentence makes you feel. Now join the X's. How do you feel?

⟵————————————⟶

bad						good
powerful						fearful
strong						weak
free						trapped
safe						unsafe
proud						ashamed
comfortable						uncomfortable
in control						out of control
happy						sad
worthless						valuable
relieved						worried
hopeful						hopeless

FOLLOW-UP EXERCISE 1.6

What have I gained, what have I lost?

AIM

To encourage the young person/people to think about the balance of gains and losses for themselves resulting from their actions that led them to being placed on this course.

APPROXIMATE TIME

5–10 mins

EQUIPMENT REQUIRED

- pens
- scales (optional)
- card (optional)
- flipchart paper (optional)

HANDOUTS NEEDED

What have I gained, what have I lost? (p.89)

Instructions

IN A ONE-TO-ONE OR GROUP SETTING

1. Using the **What have I gained, what have I lost?** handout, ask the young person/people to make a list of everything that they have gained and lost through their actions (or through the particular incident that led them to be on this course). Encourage them to go into detail.

Ask:

'Is there a change to the way people look at you?'

2. Ask the young person/people to give a weighting to each gain and loss, on a scale from 1 (small) to 5 (large).

This exercise is repeated later in the workbook to assess the gains and losses for the young person's victim and their parent/carer. Keep their scores handy.

Alternative exercise

Try using real life scales (such as scales for weighing letters, or scales for educational use). Ask the young person/people to write the gains and losses on individual pieces of card and put them onto one scale for gains and the other for losses. As above, keep the cards for the exercises later in the workbook.

WHAT HAVE I GAINED, WHAT HAVE I LOST?

Think about what you have gained from your offence. Think about what you have lost. List your gains and losses. Have you gained more than you have lost? Score each item from 1 (small) to 5 (large).

Gained	Score	Lost	Score

FOLLOW-UP EXERCISE 1.7
DVD and discussion

AIM
To explore the factors leading to crime and the choices made by those who offend.

APPROXIMATE TIME
5–15 minutes

EQUIPMENT REQUIRED
- DVD player
- 'What have I done?' DVD

HANDOUTS NEEDED
none

Module 1 of the DVD shows interviews with young people who have committed offences, talking about the factors that they feel contributed to the crime. The interviews are shown twice on the DVD, first in Section A and then again in Section B. The first time the group or participant can just listen to the extracts. On the second showing, the clips build up a picture of the factors leading to crime over an image of shattered glass. The offences and court outcomes are also indicated.

During or after showing the DVD, initiate discussion with the young person or group.

After Section A, pause the DVD when the text 'What made me do it' is displayed on the screen.

You could ask:

'What choices did they make?'

'Are any of these factors similar to the ones leading to what you did?'

Play Section B, and then ask:

'What could they have done differently?'

'What could you have done differently?'

Module I Close and evaluation

The young person should be asked to complete the evaluation questionnaire on p.194, which asks them to reflect on their experience of this session/module.

The evaluation questionnaire encourages the young person to circle some words to express how they feel at the end of the session/module. Point out that they could also choose their own.

Extension exercise: Plant a tree

It would be a lovely idea to ask the young person to plant a seed of a tree or other plant which then grows throughout the course. The tree/plant at the end could be given to the community in some way or planted in a 'garden of atonement/remorse' as a way of repairing the harm or restoring things.

Module 2
Thinking about the person I hurt

Aims of Module 2

- To allow the young person to draw on their own experiences of being a victim to engage with the feelings that victimization produces. To encourage an awareness in the young person of the impact of their crime(s) on the person they hurt.

- To explore the feelings that people who have experienced victimization may have in response to a crime.

- To encourage the young person to develop empathy with the person they hurt.

Exercises

Lead-in Exercise 2.1	Me as a victim.
Module 2 Core Exercise	What's it like being the person I hurt?
Follow-up Exercise 2.1	Being the person I hurt.
Follow-up Exercise 2.2	What has the person I hurt gained and lost?
Follow-up Exercise 2.3	A feelings graph for the person I hurt.
Follow-up Exercise 2.4	DVD and discussion.
Follow-up Exercise 2.5	A visit to A&E.
Module 2 Close and evaluation	

Remember to start each new session with a review of the previous session.

For groups: Circle Time ideas

AIM
To create consistency and allow the group to relax and get to know each other.

APPROXIMATE TIME
5–10 mins

EQUIPMENT REQUIRED

- Talking piece – e.g. a ball (optional)

SUGGESTED TOPICS

Tell us something you enjoy doing.

Who is your favourite celebrity?

Who do you look up to and admire?

What do you like doing most when it is really sunny?

LEAD-IN EXERCISE 2.1

Me as a victim

AIM

To allow the young person to draw on their own experiences of being a victim. To engage with the feelings that victimization produces.

Part I – How I felt when I was hurt by crime

APPROXIMATE TIME

5–15 minutes

EQUIPMENT REQUIRED

HANDOUTS NEEDED

Instructions

IN A ONE-TO-ONE AND GROUPWORK SETTING

1. Ask the young person to think of a time when they have been a victim. Stress that they shouldn't think of the most horrible thing that has happened to them. If they are struggling, suggest that the victimization does not have to be the result of a criminal act. If they still can't think of any time when they have been the victim of a crime, you could ask the following questions:

   'Have you ever had something stolen from school?'

   'Have you ever had something stolen from outside school?'

   'Has your home ever been broken into?'

   'Has anything you own been deliberately damaged by someone else?'

   'Has someone ever physically threatened you?'

   'Is there anywhere you won't go because of what happened?'

   'Have you been kicked or hit by someone?'

   'Have you ever had money or possessions taken from you against your will?'

'Can you think of any other crime you have been hurt by?'

'Do you know of a time when someone you know has been hurt by crime?'

2. Invite them to identify the feelings that were aroused for them when they were a victim. They don't need to go into the details of their experience; explain that what we are trying to establish are the feelings. This can simply be a discussion exercise, or you could ask them to write their thoughts down before discussing this topic.

Part 2: Where we feel emotions

APPROXIMATE TIME

5–15 minutes

EQUIPMENT REQUIRED
- wallpaper lining paper
- marker pens
- scissors (optional)
- laser jet address labels (optional)

HANDOUTS NEEDED
Me as a victim (p.99)
Template 4: Human figure (optional) (p.192)

Instructions
IN A ONE-TO-ONE SETTING

1. Ask the young person to draw a large figure on wallpaper lining paper. Alternatively, you could use **Template 4: Human figure** on p.192.

2. Talk about how we feel emotions in different parts of our bodies. For example, when we are nervous many of us feel 'butterflies' in our stomachs, or when we are angry many of us feel hot and clammy or get a headache, or when we are sad or upset many of us may cry.

3. Ask the young person to write or draw on their picture the feelings they had as a victim. The words should be placed onto the body shape where the feelings occur for the individual. If the young person is struggling with writing out the words, they could instead choose to cut out some of the statements on the **Me as a victim** handout on p.99. It is possible to buy

laser jet address labels that are A4-sized to turn the sentences into labels. If the young person has literacy issues, the exercise below, 'Extension/ homework exercise: Artwork', may be more appropriate.

IN A GROUPWORK SETTING

1. Split the group into pairs and give each pair a large sheet of lining paper.

2. Ask them to lay out the paper on the floor and ask one young person to lie on it whilst the other draws around them, and then swap.

3. Talk about how we feel emotions in different parts of our bodies. For example, when we are nervous many of us feel 'butterflies' in our stomachs, or when we are angry many of us feel hot and clammy or get a headache, or when we are sad or upset many of us may cry.

4. Ask the participants to write or draw on their picture the feelings they had as a victim. The words should be placed onto the body shape where the feelings occur for the individual. If the young person needs help with writing out the words, they could instead choose and cut out some of the statements on the **Me as a victim** handout on p.99. If any of the participants have literacy issues, the exercise below, 'Extension/homework exercise: Artwork', may be more appropriate.

Extension/homework exercise: Artwork
APPROXIMATE TIME
5–15 mins

EQUIPMENT REQUIRED
- paper
- felt tips, crayons, coloured pencils, paints, etc.
- coloured card
- glue
- scissors (optional)

HANDOUTS NEEDED
none

For this exercise, some modest art materials would be ideal. They could include paper, felt pens, crayons, pastels or paints. You might have coloured card, glue and scissors handy. However the exercise can be done simply with coloured markers if other materials are unavailable.

IN ONE-TO-ONE OR GROUPWORK

1. Start a discussion about how colours, shapes and symbols have direct meaning in the world around us and in our everyday lives. Take traffic lights as an example: the red on a traffic light means stop/danger and the green means go/safety. Red is often used to express danger or it can signify love and romance; red hearts, red roses. Colour is also used in language: 'I want to paint the town red', 'I'm feeling blue', or 'I'm in a dark mood'.

2. Ask the young person to choose a colour to represent the feeling words they placed on their bodies in 'Part 2: Where we feel emotions' above, or instead of the feeling words if you are doing this exercise instead of Part 2.

3. Once they have decided on a colour, ask what shape that feeling might look like. For example, an angry feeling shape might be pointed and spiky rather than rounded and curved.

4. If you have access to art materials, you could ask the young person to draw the shape they have just thought of, and either cut it out of appropriately coloured card and stick it on to their body shape, or draw it on to the body shape with pastels, paints, coloured pencils or marker pens. Stress that it does not matter what the end result looks like and that there are no right or wrong in this exercise. It is more about the process than the outcome.

Extension/homework exercise 2: Artwork – drawing the harm

APPROXIMATE TIME
10–30 mins

EQUIPMENT REQUIRED
- paper
- pens, coloured pencils, paints, etc.
- scissors and glue
- digital camera, digital art software (optional)
- sculpture materials (optional)

HANDOUTS NEEDED
Drawing the harm (p.100)
Template 1: Values coin (p.189)
(N.B. The young person needs to have completed the above extension exercise first.)

Instructions
IN A ONE-TO-ONE OR GROUPWORK SETTING

Any art materials that can allow the young person to experiment with painting, drawing or sculpture would be helpful here.

1. Ask the young person to look at the coloured feeling shapes they have placed on their bodies. Then, ask them to replicate their shapes in some form. For example, they could trace round their shapes or copy them freehand onto a piece of paper. (The colours are not important at this stage, just the shapes.)

2. Now ask the young person to cut out the shapes and arrange them in a pattern on a new piece of paper. When they are happy with the arrangement, ask them to stick the shapes on the page. Explain that because all the shapes they have drawn represent their feelings about themselves as a victim, the pattern they create by putting the shapes together illustrates the harm that was done to them as a victim.

3. The young person could then add colours to make the shapes into a drawing or painting that could become their 'harm shape'.

If you want help in introducing artwork to your sessions with young people or want to take it further (for example into photography, sculpture or digital artwork), explore whether there have ever been artists involved in your team, perhaps from partnership organizations.

Values

In Lead-in Exercise 1.1, the young person or group started to collect their values on coins. Crime often involves a breach of values. During this exercise keep an ear out for anything expressed by the participants that indicates that their experience of being victimized felt like an attack on their core values. If any more values come to light during this exercise, write them on a coin and add them to the pile.

✓

ME AS A VICTIM

If you need help with this exercise, cut out the words that fit how you felt to put on your picture.

I felt stressed	I was hurt
I felt powerless	I felt panic
I felt shocked	I felt devastated
I felt overwhelmed	I had emotional worries
I had practical worries	I felt vulnerable
I felt angry	I felt guilty
I felt to blame	I felt confused
I had physical effects	I felt scared
I felt humiliated	I was embarrassed
I felt judged	I couldn't cope very well
I lost my confidence	I kept reliving the incident
I felt sick	

✓

DRAWING THE HARM

Look at the coloured feeling shapes you placed on your body in the previous exercise. Trace or copy the shapes on to the paper below. Then make the shapes and colours into a pattern on a new piece of paper.

You can now use the pattern that you have just made to create a painting, drawing or sculpture. This is your 'harm shape'.

MODULE 2 CORE EXERCISE

What's it like being the person I hurt?

AIM
To encourage a heightened awareness of the range of impacts an offence can have on the person who is hurt.

APPROXIMATE TIME
10–15 mins

EQUIPMENT REQUIRED
- paper
- coloured pens, crayons, etc.

HANDOUTS NEEDED
Template 3: Thought and feelings bubbles (p.191)
Template 4: Human figure (optional) (p.192)

This exercise, which can build on the previous exercise, is designed to highlight to the young person the numerous ways their actions may have affected the person they hurt.

Instructions
IN A ONE-TO-ONE SETTING

1. Ask the young person to explain who was hurt by their actions. If it is a specific person suggest that they use the person's first name. Stop the young person if they use any derogatory terms. If they do not know the name of the person, rather than use the term 'victim' they could either make up a fictitious name or talk about 'the person I hurt' (see subsection on confidentiality on p.18). If several people were hurt, concentrate on the person who was probably most affected by what happened. Ask the young person to talk through the brief detail of their actions in relation to the person who was hurt.

2. Ask the young person to draw two pictures, one to show the person who was hurt before the incident and the other to show them after the incident. Link this to the previous Exercise, 'Lead-in Exercise 2.1: Me as a victim', when they drew themselves when they had been victims. Ask them to put in speech bubbles, thought bubbles and feelings bubbles, and explore

what the person they hurt might have been thinking, saying and feeling, both before and after the offence. They should add any physical injuries, etc. to the picture. If the young person is reluctant to draw figures, you could use the template figure on p.192 and the thought and feelings bubbles on p.191.

3. Ask them to compare these drawings with the ones of themselves as victims in the previous exercise. Discuss any similarities and differences.

IN A GROUPWORK SETTING

1. Ask the participants to explain who was hurt by their actions. If it is a specific person suggest that they use the person's first name. Stop the young person if they use any derogatory terms. If they do not know the name of the person, rather than use the term 'victim' they could either make up a fictitious name or talk about 'the person I hurt'. If several people were hurt, concentrate on the person who was probably most affected by what happened. Ask each young person to talk through the brief detail of their actions in relation to the person who was hurt.

2. Ask each young person to draw two pictures, one to show the person who was hurt before the incident and the other to show them after the incident. Link this to the previous exercise, 'Lead in Exercise 2.1 Me as a victim', when they drew themselves when they had been victims. Ask them to put in speech bubbles, thought bubbles and feelings bubbles, and explore what the person they hurt might have been thinking, saying and feeling, both before and after the offence. They should add any physical injuries, etc. to the picture. If the young person is reluctant to draw figures, you could use the template figure on p.192 and the thought and feelings bubbles on p.191.

3. Ask each of the participants to describe their pictures to the rest of the group.

4. Ask them to compare these drawings with the ones of themselves as victims in the previous exercise. Discuss any similarities and differences.

Extension/homework exercise
APPROXIMATE TIME
10–15 mins

EQUIPMENT REQUIRED
• scissors (optional)

HANDOUTS NEEDED
Impact cards (pp.104–5)
Template 4: Human figure (optional) (p.192)

This extension exercise is useful if the young person is finding it difficult to consider the range of effects of their actions on the person they hurt.

You may need to explain to the participants what the term 'post-traumatic stress disorder'[4] means, and explain that it is commonly associated with the experience of becoming the victim of crime, particularly if the person harmed doesn't receive appropriate support.

Instructions
IN A ONE-TO-ONE SETTING

1. Cut out the cards on the **Impact cards** handout on pp.104–5.

2. Spread the cards on a table. Some of the cards describe emotions, and the young person can be asked to colour the cards to indicate the colour of the emotions they describe.

3. The young person can be encouraged to consider where in the body the cards that describe emotions might be experienced and place the cards on the drawings of the person they hurt before and after the incident accordingly, or you can show the young person as you place the appropriate cards onto the drawings. The other cards could go around the outside of the figure.

IN A GROUPWORK SETTING

1. Cut out the cards on the **Impact cards** handout on pp.104–5.

2. This exercise can either be completed individually, in pairs, or as a group, using one person's drawings as an example.

3. Spread the cards on a table. Some of the cards describe emotions, and the partipicants can be asked to colour the cards to indicate the colour of the emotions they describe.

4. The participants can be encouraged to consider where in the body the cards that describe emotions might be experienced and place the cards on the drawings of the person they hurt before and after the offence accordingly, or you can show the participants as you place the appropriate cards onto the drawings. The other cards could go around the outside of the figure.

---

4   Post-traumatic stress disorder, or PTSD, is an anxiety disorder. It can happen to someone after a terrifying event or ordeal in which grave physical harm occurred or was threatened. People with PTSD have frightening thoughts and memories of their ordeal. They feel numb inside, especially with people they were once close to. They may have sleep problems, they may be easily startled and have flashbacks.

IMPACT CARDS

Injuries	Trauma of court appearance
Psychological trauma	Reliving the incident again and again
Hospital or GP visits	Difficulties coping with daily life
Feeling overwhelmed and unable to cope	Time off work
Repairs to property	Loss of money
Difficulties with transport	Seeing life differently
Doubting themself (especially if not believed)	Fear of crime in general
Lack of support	Loss of time taken to report the crime
Being blamed for being a victim	Feeling put out
Feeling guilt – could they have stopped it?	Anger
The police may have been helpful or not helpful	Shock

(continued)

IMPACT CARDS CONT.

Panic	Feeling embarrassed or humiliated
Feeling out of control and powerless	Fear of revenge
Difficulty expressing feelings	Loss of confidence
Lack of information about what was happening afterwards	Symptoms of stress, e.g. hair loss
Breakdown requiring mental health care	Ongoing fear, looking over their shoulder
Paranoia	Difficulty sleeping
Feeling devastated	Self-destructive behaviour
Post-traumatic stress disorder	Effects on relationships
Intimidation from the family of the person who offended against them	If in local news/well known, having to deal with people knowing about the incident
Insurance claim difficulties	Anxiety, panic attacks
Confusion	Feeling targeted, vulnerable
Self-harming	

FOLLOW-UP EXERCISE 2.1

Being the person I hurt

AIMS

To give the young person the opportunity to experience the perspective of the person they hurt, and explore any possible need for restoration which that person may have.

To give the young person the opportunity to think about what they might wish to do for the person they hurt.

APPROXIMATE TIME

5–15 mins

EQUIPMENT REQUIRED

- sticky name labels
- card (optional)
- pens

HANDOUTS NEEDED

Being the person I hurt (p.109)
Role play questions (p.110)
Template 1: Values coin (p.189)

Instructions

IN A ONE-TO-ONE SETTING

1. Ask the young person to play the role of the person they hurt in a role play, where you play the part of them, i.e. the person who caused the hurt. It might help to make the exercise clearer if you produce sticky name badges for both of you with the appropriate names written on.

2. Ask the questions on the **Role play questions** handout (p.110), and any other questions you think of that might be powerful.

3. Encourage the young person (still in the role of the person they hurt) to ask you questions, to answer any concerns they may have. They may like to have five minutes to think about this and write their questions down on the **Being the person I hurt** handout (p.109).

4. If the young person has committed a crime that left someone badly hurt (emotionally and/or physically), be careful to de-role them at the end. You can do this by:

- asking them to stand up and take the sticky name label off

- asking them to stick the label on the back of their chair

- asking them to now sit in your chair

- reminding them that they are not the person they hurt

- asking them to give their own name and age

- asking them whether they are ready to say goodbye to the person they hurt, and discard the label

- asking them to tell you an important difference between them and the person they hurt

- checking that they are okay, and perhaps asking them, '*What are your plans for the rest of the day?*'

5.   Ask the young person to think about whether there is anything they can do or feel they ought to do for the person they hurt. Another way of putting it might be to ask them if they think there is anything that the person they hurt needs that they might be able to help with. If they want to express this openly they can, but they don't have to.

IN A GROUPWORK SETTING

1.   Split the group up into pairs. Ask one participant from each pair to play the person they hurt in a role play, and the other should play the part of the person who hurt them. It might help to make the exercise clearer if you produce sticky name badges for both participants.

2.   The 'offender' should ask the 'person who was hurt' the questions on the role play questions handout, and any other questions they can think of that might be powerful.

3.   Encourage the 'person who was hurt' to ask their 'offender' questions, to answer any concerns they may have. They may like to have five minutes to think about this and write their questions down on the **Being the person I hurt** handout (p.109).

4.   If the young person has committed a crime that left someone badly hurt (emotionally and/or physically), be careful to de-role them at the end. See step 4 of the one-to-one instructions above.

5.   Each pair should swap roles and repeat the exercise.

6.   Ask each young person to think about whether there is anything they can do or feel they ought to do for the person they hurt. Another way of

putting it might be to ask them if they think there is anything that the person they hurt needs that they might be able to help with. If they want to express this openly they can, but they don't have to.

Values

In Lead-in Exercise 1.1, the young person or group started to collect their values on coins.

People who have been hurt by crime also have values, which may well have been breached by what was done to them. During this exercise look out for anything expressed during the role play that might illustrate a value for the person hurt by the young person's crime. If any more values come to light during this exercise, write them on a coin and add them to the pile.

BEING THE PERSON I HURT

Imagine that you are the person who was hurt by what you did. Being the person you hurt, do you have any questions that need answers?

ROLE PLAY QUESTIONS

What is your name?

How old are you?

What is the relationship between you and the person who hurt you?

What happened to you?

Now use the restorative enquiry questions:

How did you feel just before the incident?

What were you thinking at that point?

How did you feel during the incident?

What were you thinking as it was happening?

Did you say anything?

How have you felt since the incident?

What have your thoughts been since it happened?

How are you feeling now?

What are your thoughts about the incident now?

Who has the crime affected?

How has it affected you?

What do you think of the person who victimized you?

What would you have liked to say to the person who victimized you at the time of the incident?

What would you like to say to the person who victimized you now?

What would you like to ask him/her?

What would help you to move on?

Are there any needs that you still have?

FOLLOW-UP EXERCISE 2.2

What has the person I hurt gained and lost?

AIM
To encourage the young person to think about the balance of gains and losses resulting from their actions for the person they hurt.

APPROXIMATE TIME
5–10 mins

EQUIPMENT REQUIRED
- pens
- flipchart paper (optional)

HANDOUTS NEEDED
What has the person I hurt gained and lost? (p.113)

Ask the young person to repeat the exercise from the previous module 'What have I gained, what have I lost?' (Follow-up Exercise 1.6 on p.87), this time making a list of everything that the person they hurt may have gained and lost as a result of their actions. You may consider simply asking the young person to add these to the bottom of the first list. N.B. If the young person has not completed 'What have I gained, what have I lost?', this is not a problem.

Instructions
IN A ONE-TO-ONE SETTING

1. Using the **What has the person I hurt gained and lost?** handout, ask the young person to make a list of everything they think the person they hurt may have gained and lost as a result of their actions. Encourage them to go into detail.

2. Ask the young person to give a weighting to each gain and loss from 1 (small) to 5 (large).

IN A GROUPWORK SETTING

1. Using the **What has the person I hurt gained and lost?** handout or a flipchart, make a collective list for the whole group. Ask the participants to think about everything the persons they hurt may have gained and lost as a result of their actions. Encourage them to go into detail.

2. Ask the participants to give a weighting to each gain and loss from 1 (smal) to 5 (large).

WHAT HAS THE PERSON I HURT GAINED AND LOST?

List what you think the person you hurt has gained and what they have lost (e.g. insurance money, feeling safe, losing treasured possessions). Have they gained or lost from your actions? Score each item from 1 (small) to 5 (large).

Gained	Score	Lost	Score

A feelings graph for the person I hurt

AIM

To help the young person consider in depth how their actions made the person they hurt feel on the day of the incident, by charting their feelings during that day.

APPROXIMATE TIME

10–15 mins

EQUIPMENT REQUIRED

- coloured paper
- expression stickers/cut-outs
- colouring pencils, crayons, etc. (optional)
- flipchart paper (optional)
- laser jet address labels (optional)

HANDOUTS NEEDED

A feelings graph for _____ (p.116)

Following on from Lead-in Exercise 1.3: **My feelings graph** on p.46, ask the young person to imagine the changing feelings that the person they hurt may have experienced during the day on which the incident occurred, and draw a feelings graph. If known, ask them to write the person's name on their graph.

A feelings graph is a way of illustrating how our feelings change through the day. You may like to have a supply of art resources available, including coloured paper, stickers of smiley and sad faces, crayons, etc. to help the young person engage with the exercise. The cartoon faces on **Template 2: Feelings faces** on p.190 can be cut up and glued or placed onto the graph. It is also possible to buy laser jet address labels that are A4-sized to turn that page into stickers.

Instructions
IN A ONE-TO-ONE AND GROUPWORK SETTING

1. Give each participant a copy of the handout **A feelings graph for _____** on p.116, and keep a copy for yourself.

2. Explain that the vertical axis represents how the person who was hurt might have felt, with very unhappy at the bottom and very happy at the top, and the horizontal axis represents the time, from waking to bedtime.

3. Demonstrate to the young person how to fill in the graph. In drawing your own example graph, show how events during the day lead to peaks and troughs of feelings and emotions. Point out if you think there is a default position somewhere in the middle.

4. Ask the participant(s) to draw a feelings graph for the day on which the incident occurred.

5. Ask the young person to annotate the graph with the thoughts the person who was hurt may have had at different points of the day, to help establish the link between thoughts and feelings.

6. The graph can be adapted to cover the week of the incident, if significant events would otherwise be missed. Simply ask the young person to draw the graph on a sheet of flipchart paper, with each day listed on the horizontal axis.

7. Discuss how the participant(s) found the exercise and whether it produced any surprises. In a groupwork setting the young people could share their graphs in pairs and then with the whole group.

8. If the participant(s) completed Lead-in Exercise 1.3: My feelings graph on p.46, ask them to look at the two graphs for the day of the incident and think about how their day compares with the day of the person they hurt. *Are there similarities? Are there differences?*

Extension exercise

The graph could be turned into a more active exercise with the axes laid out on the floor using masking tape. The participant(s) should stand on the line in the position appropriate to the feelings of the person they hurt at a given time. You could ask the participant(s):

'How do you think they felt when they first woke up?'

'What about by mid-afternoon?'

'When they were having their dinner, how do you think they felt then?'

You could also try asking them at what point in the day they think they might have felt most sad, and at what point they felt most happy.

A FEELINGS GRAPH FOR _____

Draw a feelings graph for the person who got hurt on the day of the incident. You will have to imagine how their feelings changed through the day.

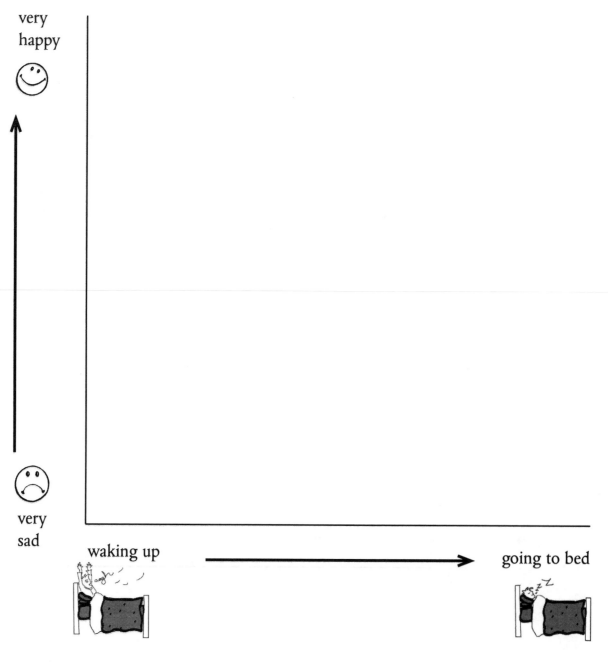

FOLLOW-UP EXERCISE 2.4

DVD and discussion

AIM

To encourage the young person to think about and discuss victim issues.

APPROXIMATE TIME

10–15 mins

EQUIPMENT REQUIRED

- DVD player

- 'What have I done?' DVD

HANDOUTS NEEDED

Module 2 Section A: What feelings does the person who got hurt have?

This section contains interviews with people who have been victimized, and who are talking about their feelings following an offence. The screen builds up a picture of the range of feelings that experiencing crime can cause.

When the screen displays the text:

'Can you work out what the crime was from the feelings?'

[Pause the DVD]

Ask the young person or group what crime might have caused each feeling on the screen.

[Play the DVD]

The screen identifies which offences caused which feeling.

The following questions come up on the screen for discussion:

1. *'Do you know how the person you hurt feels?'*

[Pause the DVD]

Ask the young person or group the question.

[Play the DVD]

2. *'Would you like to know?'*

[Pause the DVD]

Ask the young person or group the question.

[Play the DVD]

3. *'Is it important for the person committing a crime to know the feelings of the person they hurt?'*

[Pause the DVD]

Ask the young person or group the question.

[Play the DVD]

4. *'Why?'*

[Pause the DVD]

Initiate a discussion with the young person or group.

Module 2 Section B: Crimes have consequences

Section B contains extracts showing some of the consequences that crime can have for those who have been hurt.

The following questions come up on the screen to initiate a discussion with the individual or group:

'Did your offence have similar consequences for other people?'

'If so, what were the consequences?'

FOLLOW-UP EXERCISE 2.5

A visit to an Accident and Emergency Department (A&E) or meeting with a surrogate victim

APPROXIMATE TIME
1–3 hours

EQUIPMENT REQUIRED
- transport to A & E, and established links with a member of hospital staff
- arrangements made with the 'surrogate victim'

HANDOUTS NEEDED
none

If the young person committed an assault that led to physical injuries for the person who was hurt, it can be powerful to explore the physiological consequences for people who have been on the receiving end of violence.

It might be worth making contact with a health professional, who could be invited to meet the young person or group and discuss the 'after' picture they have drawn (section 2 p.101, section 2 p.102) showing the injuries they caused.

A visit to Accident & Emergency can be even more powerful if this can be arranged. The reality is that a punch, stamp or kick has the potential to maim or kill, even if that is not the intention of the attacker. Real life information about the potential dangers can be impactful.

In a similar vein, some organizations regularly invite people who have been victims of crime to speak with young people who are on a victim empathy course about their experience. Introducing young people to a 'surrogate victim' in this way can be impactful, and may be of benefit to all, if those involved haven't been able to participate in a restorative process themselves. Take care to prepare both sides thoroughly, telling them what to expect and giving time to debrief afterwards. Don't keep inviting the same people as surrogate victims – asking them to go through their experience again and again is likely to become unhelpful.

Module 2: Close and evaluation

The material the young person will have covered in this session may have left them with painful and difficult feelings. This should be acknowledged.

Allow the young person to express their feelings and assist you as their facilitator in assessing whether they need to be doing any follow-up work with anyone.

Remind the young person of the support structure they have: community, family, friends, mentor, other professionals, etc.

The young person should be asked to complete the evaluation questionnaire on p.194 for this module.

Module 3
Thinking about who else I affected

Aims of Module 3

- To encourage an awareness of the wider (ripple) effects of crime.

- To encourage the young person to think about the impact of their actions on their family and on their parent(s)/carer(s) in particular.

- To encourage the young person to think about the balance of gains and losses resulting from their actions for their families.

Exercises

Lead-in Exercise 3.1   Ripples.

Module 3 Core exercise   The ripples from my crime.

Follow-up Exercise 3.1   Role play as my parent/carer.

Follow-up Exercise 3.2   What has my family gained and lost?

Follow-up Exercise 3.3   A feelings graph for my parent(s)/carer(s).

Follow-up Exercise 3.4   DVD and discussion.

Module 3 Close and evaluation

Remember to start each new session with a review of the previous session.

For groups: Circle Time ideas

AIM

To create consistency and allow the group to relax and get to know each other.

APPROXIMATE TIME

5–10 mins

EQUIPMENT REQUIRED

- Talking piece – e.g. a ball (optional)

SUGGESTED TOPICS

What do you like doing most when it is raining?

What is your favourite place?

What reputation would you most like to have?

What do you think young people need most?

LEAD-IN EXERCISE 3.1

Ripples

AIM
To introduce the notion of the ripple effect visually.

APPROXIMATE TIME
5 mins

EQUIPMENT REQUIRED
- pebble or coin
- bowl
- some water

HANDOUTS NEEDED
none

Instructions

1. Ask the young person to drop a small object, such as a pebble, into a bowl of water.

2. Together, watch the ripples it creates. Then ask the young person the following questions:

   'How far do the ripples travel?'

   'How many ripples are there?'

   'Are you able to count them?'

   'If the bowl was bigger, how far would the ripples go?'

3. Generate a discussion. In the same way as the ripples spread out from the central point, crime has a long-term effect and spreads out to the families, friends and community of the people involved/person who caused the harm; this includes the person who was hurt, the offender and the police.

Alternative exercise

If there is a pond or lake nearby, it might be worth a trip to explore ripples on a larger stretch of water. Two small stones creating overlapping ripples could represent the ripples for the young person and the person they hurt, spreading out to their respective networks. The ripples could be photographed.

MODULE 3 CORE EXERCISE

The ripples from my crime

AIM

For the young person to identify all of the people affected by their crime.

APPROXIMATE TIME

10–15 mins

EQUIPMENT REQUIRED

- paper
- pens
- pebbles (optional)
- news/magazine clippings (optional)

HANDOUTS NEEDED

Instructions

IN A ONE-TO-ONE SETTING

1. On a blank piece of paper, ask the young person to draw concentric circles like the ripples in the previous exercise. The paper represents a pond.

2. Ask the young person to work from the centre and write in all of the people who have been adversely affected by their actions (or alternatively place objects such as pebbles on the picture to represent those people). Those most seriously affected should be placed in the centre, with those less badly affected in the outer circle. Encourage broad thinking – so as to include those individuals that may not be obvious, for example nurses in the Accident & Emergency Department, parents, grandparents, police and the wider community who may not be direct victims.

3. If the young person is struggling, a scenario or case study could be used, for example from the day's newspapers.

4. When they have finished doing the drawing, it should represent many of those who have been affected by what the young person did.

5. Now engage the young person in a discussion about how these people will have been affected. Encourage them to distinguish between immediate,

medium and longer term effects. Discuss the young person's thinking in placing people nearer or further away from the centre.

IN A GROUPWORK SETTING

1. Clear a large area in the middle of the room. Mark several concentric circles on the floor using masking tape to represent the ripples. Explain that the middle of the smallest circle represents the crime.

2. Ask one of the young people to start identifying all the people affected by their crime (including themselves). Nominate other young people in the group to represent each person affected, and ask them to stand at a spot on the floor, nearer or further from the crime as directed by the young person. Those most seriously affected should be placed in the centre, with those less badly affected in the outer circle. Encourage broad thinking – so as to include those individuals that may not be obvious. Ask the young person to include witnesses, police officers, the general public, grand parents, siblings – anyone whose lives were touched to a larger or smaller extent.

3. When everyone is in place, tell them to imagine that they are the person they are representing, and ask them in turn:

   'Say a few words about what you felt about the crime.'

   'How were you affected?'

   'What was the hardest thing about that experience?'

Extension/homework exercise
APPROXIMATE TIME
10 mins–1½ hours

EQUIPMENT REQUIRED

- art equipment such as coloured pens, crayons, coloured card, paints, sculpture clay, wire, ink, etc.

- digital camera, digital artwork software (optional)

HANDOUTS NEEDED
The ripples from my crime (optional) (p.127)

Ask the young person to try to capture the ripple effect in a more creative way. For example they could:

- draw it

- paint it

- make a sculpture of it

- create a wire mobile in a spiral shape

- photograph it on a digital camera and download it on to a computer

- use paper marbling inks in a bowl of water: drop a small object in and print off the ripple effect as it is happening by laying a sheet of thick paper onto the surface of the water.

THE RIPPLES FROM MY CRIME

Draw ripples in some way. Draw all the people affected by your crime. Those most affected go near the centre. Those least affected go near the edge.

Role play as my parent/carer

AIM
To encourage the young person to think about the impact of their actions on their parent/carer.

APPROXIMATE TIME
5–15 mins

EQUIPMENT REQUIRED
- sticky name labels
- marker pens
- pens

HANDOUTS NEEDED
Impact role play (p.131)

Although this Module emphasizes the impact of their actions on the young person's parent(s) or carer(s) it is important to explore the effect on their siblings too. Sometimes a younger brother or sister can become distressed, becoming convinced that their older sibling will be sent to prison even for a minor offence. They may also try to emulate the offending behaviours, or feel responsible, disappointed or let down. The exercises in this module can all be repeated with the sibling in mind.

For many young people, a grandparent, uncle or aunt could be a significant person, and it may be most appropriate for this person to be the subject of the role play rather than a parent.

Instructions
IN A ONE-TO-ONE SETTING

1. Ask the young person to play the role of their parent(s)/carer(s) in a role play, where you play the part of them as the person who offended. It might help to make the exercise clearer if you produce sticky name badges for both of you with the appropriate names written on. To get into role ask them:

   'What's your name?'

'How old are you?'

'How many children do you have?'

'How long have you been a parent/carer?'

2. Ask the questions on the **Impact role play** handout on p.131, and any other questions you think of that might be powerful.

3. Encourage the young person (still in the role of their parent/carer) to ask you questions, to answer any concerns they may have. They may like to have five minutes to think about this and write their questions down on the **Impact role play** handout.

4. Ask the young person to come out of role play by saying what their name is and how old they are. If the young person has become deeply involved in this role and needs further de-roling, see step 4 of Follow-up Exercise 2.1 on p.106.

5. Ask the young person:

    'What was it like to be your parent/carer?'

    'What feeling was the strongest for you?'

    'What did you learn about how they may have felt?'

    'What do you view differently now?'

IN A GROUPWORK SETTING

1. Either split the group into pairs, or (and this may work better) take each young person through the role play in turns in front of the group.

2. Ask the young person to play the role of their parent(s)/carer(s) in a role play, where you play the part of them as the person who offended. It might help to make the exercise clearer if you produce sticky name badges for both of you with the appropriate names written on. To get into role ask them:

    'What's your name?'

    'How old are you?'

    'How many children do you have?'

    'How long have you been a parent/carer?'

3. Ask the questions on the **Impact role play** handout on p.131, and any other questions you think of that might be powerful.

4. Encourage the young person (still in the role of their parent/carer) to ask you questions, to answer any concerns they may have. They may like to have five minutes to think about this and write their questions down on the **Impact role play** handout.

5. Ask the young person to come out of role play by saying what their name is and how old they are. If the young person has become deeply involved in this role and needs further de-roling, see step 4 of Follow-up Exercise 2.1 on p.106.

6. Ask the young person:

   'What was it like to be your parent/carer?'

   'What feeling was the strongest for you?'

   'What did you learn about how they may have felt?'

   'What do you view differently now?

7. Ask the whole group to say what they have learnt from this exercise.'

IMPACT ROLE PLAY

Impact on my parent/carer

Imagine that you are your parent/carer. Do you have any questions that need answers?

Questions

- How did you find out about the incident?

- Where were you?

- Who were you with?

- What did you think at the time?

- What did it feel like going to the police station/court?

- What do you think about the whole experience now?

- How do you feel about your son/daughter now?

- Who else has been affected?

- Has the incident had any effect on how you see the future?

What has my family gained and lost?

AIM

To encourage the young person to think about the balance of gains and losses resulting from their actions for their families.

APPROXIMATE TIME

5–10 mins

EQUIPMENT REQUIRED

- pens
- scales (optional)
- card

HANDOUTS NEEDED

What has my family gained and lost? (p.134)
Was it worth it? (p.135)

Part I

Ask the young person to repeat the exercise from Follow-up Exercise 1.6 and Follow-up Exercise 2.2, this time making a list of everything that their family may have gained and lost as a result of their actions. As before, you may like to simply keep on adding to the bottom of the original list, and in a groupwork setting a collective list for the whole group is a possibility. If the young person has not completed either of the previous exercises, this is not a problem.

Instructions

IN A ONE-TO-ONE OR GROUPWORK SETTING

1. Using the **What has my family gained and lost?** handout on p.134, ask the young person to make a list of everything their family has gained and lost through their actions (or through the particular incident that led them to be on this course). Encourage them to go into detail.

2. Ask the young person to give a weighting to each gain and loss, on a scale from 1 (small) to 5 (large).

If the young person completed Follow-up Exercise 1.6 and Follow-up Exercise 2.2, look through the scores for the previous two gains and losses exercises with the young person. Ask them to add up all of the scores to give a total for gains and a total for losses.

Part 2
Was it worth it?

Using the grids in the handout **Was it worth it?** on p.135, ask the young person to colour the appropriate number of squares to indicate the benefits and costs of the incident to all those who have been affected, including themselves, the person they hurt and their families. Initiate a discussion about whether the offence was, on balance, worth it.

✓

WHAT HAS MY FAMILY GAINED AND LOST?

Think about what your friends and family have gained or lost from your actions. Have they gained or lost? Score each item from 1 (small) to 5 (large).

Gained	Score	Lost	Score

WAS IT WORTH IT?

Colour in the squares for each thing that has been gained and lost by your crime. Use the scores that your case holder has kept. *Was it worth it?*

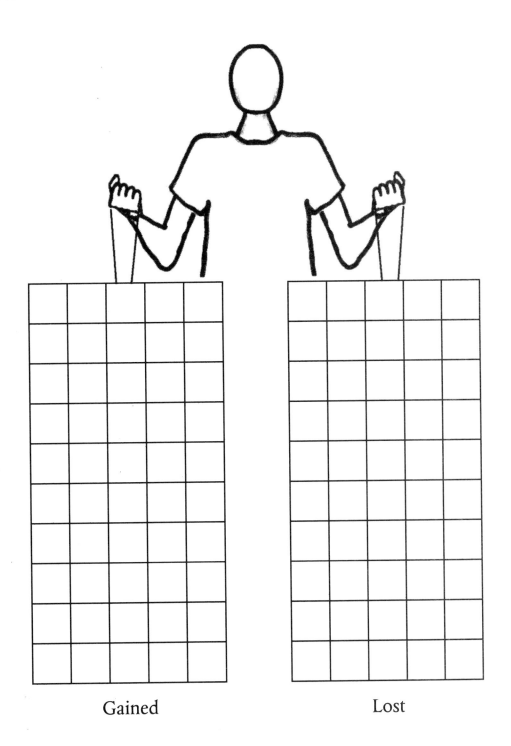

Gained   Lost

A feelings graph for my parent(s)/carer(s)

AIM

To help the young person consider how their actions made their parent(s)/carer(s) feel on the day of the incident that led to the young person being placed on the course by charting their feelings during that day.

APPROXIMATE TIME

10–15 mins

EQUIPMENT REQUIRED

- coloured paper
- expression stickers/cut-outs
- crayons
- flipchart paper (optional)
- laser jet address labels (optional)

HANDOUTS NEEDED

A feelings graph for my parent(s)/carer(s) (p.138)
Template 2: Feelings faces (p.190) (optional)

Following on from Lead-in Exercise 1.3 and Follow-up Exercise 2.3, ask the young person to imagine the changing feelings that their parent(s)/carer(s) may have experienced during the day of the incident (or if different, the day that they learnt about the incident) and draw a feelings graph. Ask them to write the person's name on their graph. You may like to have a supply of art resources available, including coloured paper, stickers of smiley and sad faces, crayons, etc. to help the young person engage with the exercise. The cartoon faces on **Template 2: Feelings faces** on p.190 can be cut up and glued or placed onto the graph. It is also possible to buy laser jet address labels that are A4-sized to turn that page into stickers.

Instructions

IN A ONE-TO-ONE AND GROUPWORK SETTING

1. Give each participant a copy of **A feelings graph for my parent(s)/carer(s)** on p.138, and keep a copy for yourself.

2.   Explain that the vertical axis represents how the young person's parent(s)/carer(s) felt, with very unhappy at the bottom and very happy at the top, and the horizontal axis represents the time, from waking to bedtime.

3.   Demonstrate to the young person how to fill in the graph. In drawing your own example graph, show how events during the day lead to peaks and troughs of feelings and emotions. Point out if you think there is a default position somewhere in the middle.

4.   Ask the participant(s) to draw a feelings graph for the day of the incident that led to them being on this course (or for one of the incidents if there were several).

5.   Ask the young person to annotate the graph with the thoughts their parent(s)/carer(s) may have had at different points of the day, to help establish the link between thoughts and feelings.

6.   The graph can be adapted to cover the week of the incident, if significant events would otherwise be missed. Simply ask the young person to draw the graph on a sheet of flipchart paper, with each day listed on the horizontal axis.

7.   Discuss how they found the exercise and whether it produced any surprises. In a groupwork setting the young people could share their graphs in pairs and then with the whole group.

8.   If all three of the feelings graphs have been completed, they can be compared:

     'Looking at your three feelings graphs for your offence, how did your day compare with the day of the person you hurt, and of your parent/carer? Are there similarities? Are there differences?'

A FEELINGS GRAPH FOR MY PARENT(S)/CARER(S)

Draw a feelings graph for your parent/carer on the day of your offence. You will have to imagine how their feelings changed through the day.

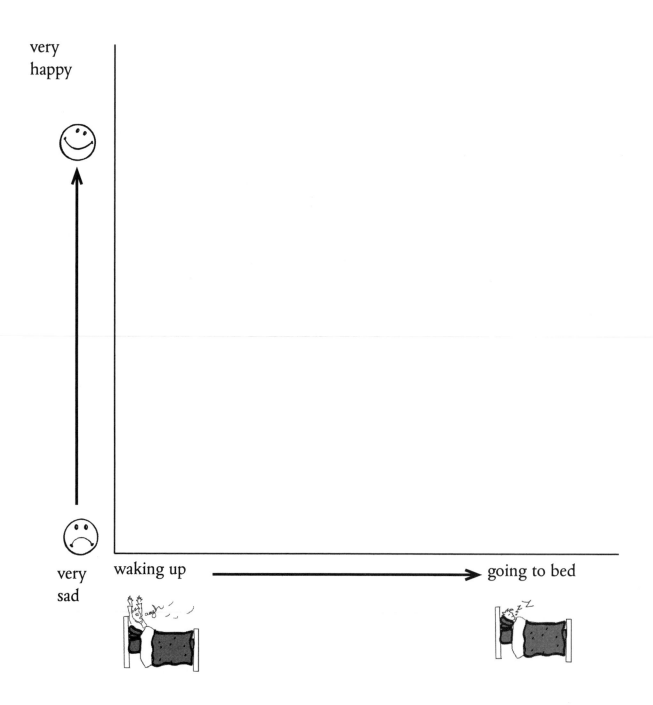

FOLLOW-UP EXERCISE 3.4

DVD and discussion

AIM
To encourage the young person to consider who else is affected by crime.

APPROXIMATE TIME
5–15 mins

EQUIPMENT REQUIRED
- DVD player
- 'What have I done?' DVD

HANDOUTS NEEDED
none

Module 3 of the DVD considers the wider consequences of crime and the 'ripple effect', using similar imagery to that developed in Lead-in Exercise 3.1 on p.123 and Module 3 Core Exercise on p.124.

After each person being interviewed speaks, the text on the screen indicates who else has been affected by the crime, showing how the consequences of an offence ripple out.

After the extracts the following questions are displayed on the screen to initiate a discussion with the young person or group:

'Did your offence have consequences for other people?'

'Who else was affected?'

Module 3 Close and evaluation
The young person should be asked to complete the evaluation questionnaire on p.193 which asks them to reflect on their experience of this module.

The evaluation questionnaire encourages the young person to circle some words to express how they feel at the end of the session. Point out that they could also choose their own.

Module 4
My chance to put things right

Aims of Module 4

- To summarize the previous modules with an overview of the causes and consequences of crime.

- To illustrate that positive things that happen in the life of the young person can have beneficial consequences for others.

- To explore the needs of the person that was hurt, and start the young person thinking about what they might do for that person.

- To explore ways for the young person to be able to make amends to the person they hurt, to that person's family and to their communities.

- To encourage the young person to look forward and make a commitment to avoid offending in future.

- To consolidate the young person's understanding of restorative justice.

Exercises

Lead-in Exercise 4.1	My conflict tree.
Module 4 Core Exercise	Crime tears people apart – what can help to put them back together?
Follow-up Exercise 4.1	Letter to the person I hurt.
Follow-up Exercise 4.2	Letter from the person I hurt.
Follow-up Exercise 4.3	Persuade the person I hurt.
Follow-up Exercise 4.4	DVD and discussion.
Follow-up Exercise 4.5	My harmony tree.
Follow-up Exercise 4.6	What makes a good role model?
Follow-up Exercise 4.7	What others think of me.
Follow-up Exercise 4.8	The Martians have landed!

Follow-up Exercise 4.9   Looking to the future.

Follow-up Exercise 4.10   Explain restorative justice to someone new.

Module 4 Close and evaluation.

Remember to start each new session with a review of the previous session.

For groups: Circle Time ideas

AIM
To create consistency and allow the group to relax and get to know each other.

APPROXIMATE TIME
5–10 mins

EQUIPMENT REQUIRED
- Talking piece – e.g. a ball (optional)

SUGGESTED TOPICS

What qualities do you most admire in other people?

What is your favourite sport?

What is your favourite film?

Who makes you laugh the most?

LEAD-IN EXERCISE 4.1

My conflict tree

AIMS

To summarize the previous modules with an overview of the causes and consequences of crime.

To encourage the young person to explore all the root causes of their actions that led them to being on this course and their consequences in a pictorial way.

APPROXIMATE TIME

10–30 mins

EQUIPMENT REQUIRED

- pens

HANDOUTS NEEDED

My conflict tree (p.145)

In previous exercises that involve artwork, we have included a handout or template to use if the young person is not artistic. However, in our experience, every young person can draw a tree, and it is always preferable not to be too prescriptive.

Instructions

IN A ONE-TO-ONE AND GROUPWORK SETTING

1. Ask the young person to draw the trunk of a tree on the **My conflict tree** handout (p.145).

2. Ask them to write or draw in or next to the trunk one word or a one line description of what they did, for example 'burglary'.

3. Then ask them to draw in the roots of the tree and for each of the roots to write or draw a root cause of what they did.

4. Reflecting on the exercises in Modules 2 and 3 where they explored responsibility and consequences, ask them to draw leaves, each of which represents a consequence of their actions, which might be for:

    - themselves

    - the person they hurt

    - their family

    - the family of the person they hurt

- their wider community

- the wider community of the person they hurt.

5.   Challenge any sign of the five examples of defensive thinking (from Module 1 Follow-up Exercise 1.1, p.58).

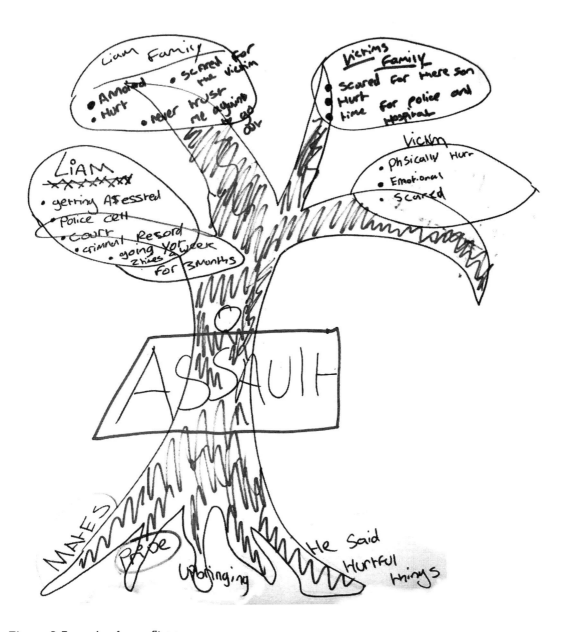

Figure 3 Example of a conflict tree

Extension/homework exercise 1: Artwork
APPROXIMATE TIME

10 mins–1½ hours

EQUIPMENT REQUIRED
- coloured pencils, crayons, paints, felt tips, etc.
- coloured paper, coloured tissue, fabric
- glue
- scissors

HANDOUTS NEEDED

Create a conflict tree using art materials, potentially producing an art piece that could be given as a gift to the person who was hurt, a 'surrogate victim' or community representative. Consider framing it, and having a written or typed explanation to accompany the picture.

Extension exercise 2: Other conflict trees
APPROXIMATE TIME

10–30 mins

EQUIPMENT REQUIRED
- pens
- paper

HANDOUTS NEEDED

The conflict tree is a powerful exercise that can be used to explore other issues and conflicts by putting them at the centre, or trunk of the issue – for example gang culture, family issues, bullying, etc. You could pick any of these topics if you feel they are relevant and worth exploring with the participant(s).

MY CONFLICT TREE

Draw the trunk of a tree. Write one word or line next to it to describe your offence. Draw roots for the tree, writing a root cause of what you did in each root. Now draw leaves. In each leaf write how your actions affected yourself and other people.

Crimes tear people apart – what can help to put them back together?

AIM

To explore the needs of the person who was hurt, and start the young person thinking about what they might do to help them in their recovery.

APPROXIMATE TIME

15–20 mins

EQUIPMENT REQUIRED

- pens

HANDOUTS NEEDED

What do people hurt by crime need? (pp.151–2)
Crime tears people apart – what can help put them back together? (p.153)
Jigsaw pieces (p.154)

This exercise is based around creating a jigsaw of the individual that the young person hurt, with the notion of putting them back together again and making them whole.

Instructions

IN A ONE-TO-ONE SETTING

1. Give the young person a copy of the handout **What do people hurt by crime need?** (pp.151–2) and the **Crime tears people apart – what can help put them back together?** handout on p.153.

2. Ask the young person to read the **What do people hurt by crime need?** handout and then write the name of the person they hurt at the top of **Crime tears people apart – what can help put them back together?**

3. Encourage the young person to come up with a list of four questions or issues that this person may need to resolve following the crime, such as 'are you sorry?', or fear of being in the house alone, etc. (If there is no

information available about their real needs, this exercise will be at least partly hypothetical.)

4. The outline has five jigsaw shapes on different parts of the body of the person hurt, which includes one small shape too many. This is because it may not be possible to repair all of the harm caused by the incident (for example, you can't remove a painful memory). You could also explain to the young person that the jigsaw shapes only cover part of the body to indicate that the experience of victimization is only one aspect of that person's life.

5. Ask the young person to write the four issues directly onto the picture inside or near the jigsaw shapes. Each jigsaw piece shaped hole therefore represents a need. You could discuss where in their body the person they hurt might feel the need (e.g. anxiety might be felt in the stomach, fear in the heart, questions in the head, etc.).

6. The young person now cuts out the four jigsaw shapes on p.154, to give the person who was hurt the 'pieces' that will go over the 'holes' to complete their jigsaw.

7. The young person has to provide an answer or consider something that could be done that might resolve each one of the questions or needs for the person they hurt. Every time they find a resolution for one of the needs, they can write the answer onto the appropriate jigsaw piece, and slot it into the correct place on the outline. Stress that some of the 'answers' will be things they might be able to do (like offer reassurance if the person is scared), whilst others will, it is hoped, be sorted out by others (like the dentist or insurance).

8. Always leave the smallest piece as a gap to indicate that one piece will never fit – we can never put it right completely.

IN A GROUPWORK SETTING

This exercise could be done first individually or in pairs followed by a discussion of the issues raised, or as a more general exercise in which the needs of all the people hurt by the group are identified on one jigsaw, followed by a collective exercise for addressing those needs.

1. Give each young person a copy of **What do people hurt by crime need?** (pp.151–2) and the **Crime tears people apart – what can help put them back together?** handout from p.153.

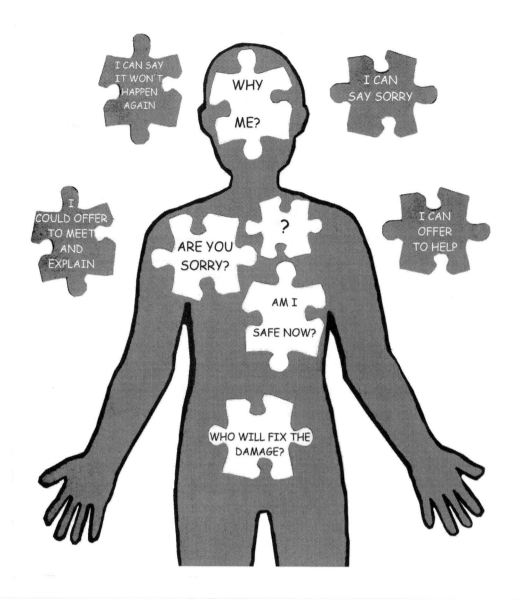

Figure 4 Example jigsaw

2. Ask the young person to read the **What do people hurt by crime need?** handout and then write the name of the person they hurt at the top of **Crime tears people apart – what can put them back together?**

3. Encourage each young person to come up with a list of four questions or issues that this person may need to resolve following the crime, such as 'are you sorry?', or 'fear of being in the house alone', etc. (If there is no information available about their real needs, this exercise will be at least partly hypothetical.)

4. The outline has five jigsaw shapes on different parts of the body of the person hurt, which includes one small shape too many. This is because it may not be possible to repair all of the harm caused by the offence (for

example, you can't remove a painful memory). You could also explain to the young person that the jigsaw shapes only cover part of the body to indicate that the experience of victimization is only one aspect of that person's life.

5.   Ask the young person to write the four issues directly onto the picture inside or near the jigsaw shapes. Each jigsaw piece shaped hole therefore represents a need. You could discuss where in their body the person they hurt might feel the need (e.g. anxiety might be felt in the stomach, fear in the heart, questions in the head, etc.).

6.   The young person now cuts out the four jigsaw shapes on p.154, to give the person who was hurt the 'pieces' that will go over the 'holes' to complete their jigsaw.

7.   The young person has to provide an answer or consider something that could be done that might resolve each one of the questions or needs for the person they hurt. Every time they find a resolution for one of the needs, they can write the answer onto the appropriate jigsaw piece, and slot it into the correct place on the outline. Stress that some of the 'answers' will be things they might be able to do (like offer reassurance if the person is scared), whilst others will, it is hoped, be sorted out by others (like the dentist or insurance).

8.   Always leave the smallest piece as a gap to indicate that one piece will never fit – we can never put it right completely.

Alternative exercise
APPROXIMATE TIME
5–10 mins

EQUIPMENT REQUIRED
*   Jenga/wooden blocks
*   paper/flipchart paper

HANDOUTS NEEDED
none

Caution: Jenga is a game, and intended to be fun. Because this exercise is dealing with issues and difficulties facing real people, it should be done with some degree of seriousness, although the playful and visual aspects of the exercise can potentially help with learning. Use your judgement in deciding whether it is likely to be helpful and appropriate, or risk trivializing the issues it intends to address.

Instructions

IN A ONE-TO-ONE AND GROUPWORK SETTING

Instead of a jigsaw, this exercise could use a set of wooden or Jenga blocks.

1. Start off with a full tower of blocks.

2. Ask each young person to identify the needs of the person they have hurt. For each need they should remove a block from the tower, stating the need as they do so. Record the needs on a piece of paper or flipchart. In a group situation, each participant should take it in turns to take a block. The tower should not collapse, but the increasing instability should indicate that people become fragile through being victimized. You could also point out that many people who have been victimized already have lots of issues and problems in their lives, which could mean that there are other pieces missing, making them fragile before the incident even occurred. Rather than placing the removed blocks back onto the tower, these should be put to one side.

3. Now ask the person carefully to replace the blocks into the gaps in the tower. For each block, ask them to indicate what will help to address the needs identified above. In this way they will be strengthening the person they hurt through their own actions.

Extension exercise 1

The main jigsaw exercise or the alternative Jenga exercise could be repeated with the young person in mind, to help them to identify their needs – what is missing in their own lives – and to explore what might help to fill those gaps to make them more complete.

Extension exercise 2: Role reversal

Following on from the role reversal in Follow-up Exercise 3.1 on p.128, role play being the young person whilst they role play being the person who was hurt in the incident. The young person, in the role of the person they hurt, asks for what they need or would like to help them move forward. This can also be done in pairs in a group setting.

Always remember to de-role the young person after any role play exercises.

WHAT DO PEOPLE HURT BY CRIME NEED?

Howard Zehr, widely recognized as a major restorative justice pioneer, has identified five categories of victims' needs:

- The need to feel safe.

- Information and answers to their questions; an explanation.

- The chance to tell their story and to be acknowledged.

- The need to be back in control.

- Something to put things back in balance – a gift or apology.

Examples of specific questions or issues that a person hurt by crime may have include:

Will I get my goods back – all of them?

Where is my car?

Will I get any insurance?

I feel nervous coming home at night – will you do it again?

Why did you do it?

Why did it happen to me – was I targeted?

Are you sorry for what happened?

Will you do this to anyone else?

Do you know how this has affected me and my family?

Is my family safe from you?

What happened to the stuff you took?

WHAT DO PEOPLE HURT BY CRIME NEED? CONT.

Restorative suggestions include:

    Answers to questions

    A verbal apology

    A letter of apology

    Meeting with the person who did it

    Hospital treatment

    Transport

    An explanation for why the offence happened

    Practical repair work

    Artwork/gift for the victim

    Reassurance that it won't happen again

    Compensation payments

    Listening to the victim's story and hearing how it has been for them

    Counselling

CRIME TEARS PEOPLE APART – WHAT CAN HELP PUT THEM BACK TOGETHER?

Write the name of the person you hurt at the top. Label each missing jigsaw piece with something they may now need following the crime. Leave the little one blank.

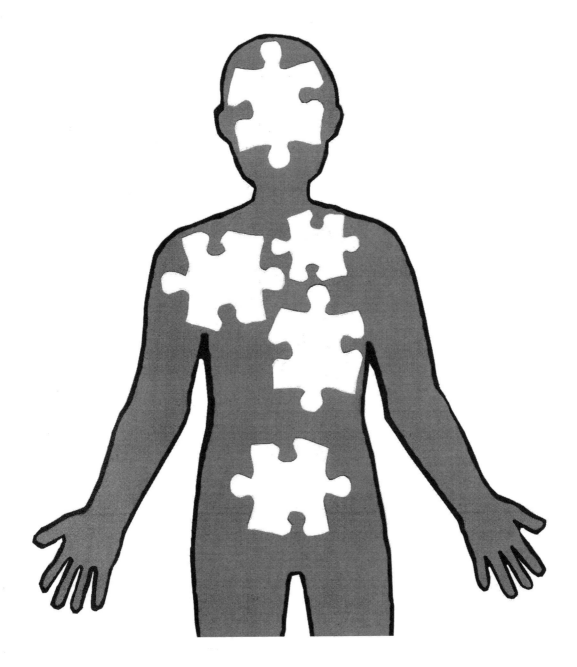

JIGSAW PIECES

Cut out these pieces to fill the gaps in your jigsaw. Write down on the pieces ideas about what might help the person you hurt with their needs so that they can move forward.

FOLLOW-UP/HOMEWORK EXERCISE 4.1

Letter to the person I hurt

AIM
To help the young person have a heightened awareness of the feelings experienced by those they have hurt, acknowledging the harm caused.

APPROXIMATE TIME
20 mins–2 hours

EQUIPMENT REQUIRED
- scrap paper
- pen
- video equipment (optional)

HANDOUTS NEEDED
Letter to _____ (p.158)
Tips for writing your letter (p.159)

This exercise could also take the form of a video apology, if the young person has literacy issues, or would prefer to express themselves that way.

Instructions
IN A ONE-TO-ONE AND GROUP SETTING

1. Encourage the young person to write a letter to the person they hurt (be sure to explain whether this will be passed on to that person, or whether it is purely an exercise to acknowledge the harm caused).

2. Explain that people who have experienced crime often want to understand why the crime happened to them, and they should consider this when writing the letter as well as what the possible effects may have been upon those hurt. Some may wish to write the letter within the session itself whilst others may prefer to write it in their own time and bring it with them, to their next session. Have lots of scrap paper available for ideas and drafts.

3. This exercise needs to be done in a way that would be meaningful to the recipient if they were to receive the letter. The letter must relate to that person's needs and interests. The letter should be the young person's own but any help they need should be available.

If the letter is to be offered to the person hurt during the incident, it is best practice for a facilitator to take the letter round in person, rather than sending it in the post. Someone (not necessarily the young person's case worker) needs to ask the person hurt if they would like to receive such a letter. Many youth offending services have arrangements for a restorative justice worker to do this liaison work and take the letter round.

It is impossible to predict how the person who got hurt will react to the letter, and whether they will recognize that the young person regrets their actions or not. During the meeting, whoever is delivering it can describe the background to the writing of the letter, and address any questions or concerns. They can ask the recipient if they would like to respond in any way.

Alternative exercise

APPROXIMATE TIME
10–30 mins

EQUIPMENT REQUIRED
none

HANDOUTS NEEDED
none

This alternative exercise is recommended if any of the participants have literacy issues.

Instructions

IN A ONE-TO-ONE OR GROUPWORK SETTING

1. Ask the young person to think about what they would say to the victim if they were given the chance.

2. Ask them what they think the person they hurt would ask them and the answers they would give.

Extension exercise

APPROXIMATE TIME
20 mins–2 hours

EQUIPMENT REQUIRED
- pen
- paper

HANDOUTS NEEDED
Letter to _____ (p.158)
Tips for writing your letter (p.159)

Acknowledging that the young person's family may have been profoundly affected by their actions, the participant(s) may like to write a letter to their parent(s)/carer(s).

✓

LETTER TO _____

TIPS FOR WRITING YOUR LETTER

A letter of apology should be in the young person's own handwriting and can include the following:

- A meaningful greeting.

- A statement that the recipient has a choice about reading the letter or not.

- An explanation about what you did and why you did it.

- A statement of responsibility for the incident, e.g. 'it was my fault, not yours.'

- How you think your behaviour has affected the person you hurt and made their life difficult. Who else has been affected?

- A statement about your acceptance of help from others to help prevent a repeat of the incident and what you are doing to put your life to rights and stay out of trouble.

- A statement of hope about the recovery and future of those you hurt.

- Addressing any concerns, particularly relating to the need for the person you hurt to feel safe.

- A description of what Order you are on.

- If possible, what do you think could be done to repair the harm caused?

FOLLOW-UP/HOMEWORK EXERCISE 4.2

Letter from the person I hurt

AIM

To help the young person see the point of view of the person they hurt.

APPROXIMATE TIME

15 mins–2hours

EQUIPMENT REQUIRED

- paper
- pen
- computer and printer (optional)

HANDOUTS NEEDED

Letter from _____ (p.162)
Tips for writing a letter from the person you hurt (p.163)
You may be able to use information from victim reports or personal statements (if they are in the public domain).

Instructions

IN A ONE-TO-ONE SETTING

Give the participant a copy of **Letter from _____** on (p.162).

1. Ask the young person to pretend that they are the person that they hurt.

2. Ask them to write a letter to themselves as if it came from the person they hurt (or that person's parents).

3. Discuss with the young person whether they are writing the letter as if it is in response to their own letter, or as an initiative from the person they hurt.

4. Use extra paper if needed. Refer to the notes on 'Terminology' (p.15) re: using a personal or fictitious name.

IN A GROUPWORK SETTING

1. Give each participant a copy of **Letter from _____** on (p.162).

2. Ask the young person to pretend that they are the person that they hurt.

3. Ask them to write a letter to themselves as if it came from the person they hurt (or that person's parents).

4. You might give each participant a choice about whether they are writing the letter as if it is in response to their own letter, or as an initiative from the person they hurt.

5. Use extra paper if needed. Refer to the notes on 'Terminology' (p.15) re: using a personal or fictitious name.

6. If appropriate, the letters could be shared with the group.

✓

LETTER FROM _____

Dear _____ (your name)

TIPS FOR WRITING A LETTER FROM THE PERSON YOU HURT

It should cover:

1. How that person felt about what happened at the time.

2. How they feel now.

3. Who else has been affected and how.

4. How they feel about you.

5. What they would want to happen (to you, to them)

Consider anything else you think the person would want to say to you. Think this through carefully. Make some notes first and then write the letter.

Persuade the person I hurt

AIM

To explore why some people who have experienced crime might choose to engage in a restorative process and others won't.

APPROXIMATE TIME

5–15 mins

EQUIPMENT REQUIRED

*   sticky name labels (optional)

HANDOUTS NEEDED

Try to avoid using the term 'victim' for this exercise. Use the person's real name if you know it. If not, you could consider choosing a fictitious name.

Instructions

IN A ONE-TO-ONE SETTING

1. Ask the young person to play the role of the person they hurt in a role play, where you play the part of them as the person who offended. It might help to make the exercise clearer if you produce sticky name badges for both of you with the appropriate names written on.

2. Tell them to voice all the reasons why, as the person hurt, they would choose not to meet up with you (the young person who hurt them). Then ask the young person to give all the reasons in favour of meeting up.

3. Be careful to de-role them at the end (see p.106).

IN A GROUPWORK SETTING

1. Split the group into pairs. Ask one participant from each pair to play the person they hurt in a role play, and the other should play the part of the person who offended. It might help to make the exercise clearer if you produce sticky name badges for both participants.

2. The participant role playing the person who was hurt should voice all the reasons why, as the person hurt, they would choose not to meet up with the young person who hurt them. Then ask the other role player to give all the reasons in favour of meeting up.

3. Be careful to de-role them at the end (see p.106).

DVD and discussion

AIM

To explore the benefits of a restorative approach by hearing about the experience of some people who have been through the process.

APPROXIMATE TIME

5–10 minutes

EQUIPMENT REQUIRED

- DVD player
- 'What have I done?' DVD

HANDOUTS NEEDED

Module 4 of the DVD explores how people who have experienced crime may benefit from a meeting with the person who hurt them, by showing interviews of people who have been through, or are about to go through, a restorative meeting. As the people are speaking, the text on the screen reinforces the benefit that they have identified.

After the interviews the following question is shown on the screen to initiate discussion with the young person or group:

'Why might the person you hurt like to meet with you?'

FOLLOW-UP EXERCISE 4.5

My harmony tree

AIM
To illustrate that positive things that happen in the life of the young person can have beneficial consequences for themselves and others.

APPROXIMATE TIME
10–30 mins

EQUIPMENT REQUIRED
- paper
- pens

HANDOUTS NEEDED
My harmony tree (p.169)
Template 1: Values coin (p.189)
In the same way that crime can create a vicious spiral of negative consequences that ripple out from the incident, positive changes in the life of the young person who offended can create a positive spiral for themselves and others. This exercise is similar to Lead-in Exercise 4.1: My conflict tree, but focuses on the positive actions the young person could perform to improve their life path.

Values

In Lead-in Exercise 1.1, the young person or group started to collect their values on coins. This exercise may highlight positive values that the young person or group aspire to or are living up to in their lives.

Instructions
IN A ONE-TO-ONE OR GROUPWORK SETTING

1. Ask the young person to draw the trunk of a tree on the **My harmony tree** handout.

2. Ask the young person to write one sentence in or next to the trunk to describe something in their life that they could do (or perhaps that they have already done) that is really positive. It could be something as simple as 'staying out of trouble' or 'going to school'.

3. Ask them to draw roots for the tree, and write one thing that would help to make the positive change happen in each root. Now they should draw leaves, and in each leaf write how that positive change would affect themselves and others.

Trunk: Leaf: Leaf:

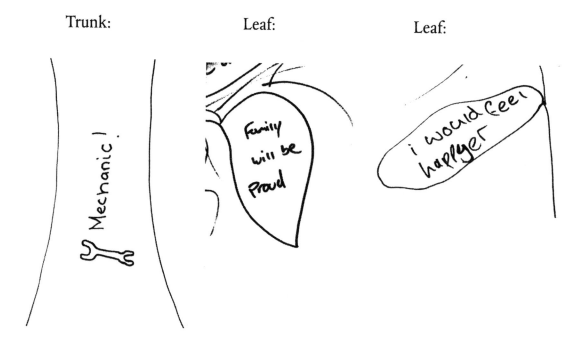

Figure 5 Details from example harmony trees

Extension/homework exercise
APPROXIMATE TIME
10 mins–1½ hours

EQUIPMENT REQUIRED
*   paper
*   paints, felt tips, oil pastels, crayons, etc.
*   fabric, coloured paper, tissue, etc.
*   glue
*   scissors (optional)

HANDOUTS NEEDED
none

The harmony tree could also be turned into a work of art, and potentially presented to the person who was hurt to show how the young person is turning their life around.

MY HARMONY TREE

Draw the trunk of a tree. Now write one word or line next to it. It can describe something in your life that you could do that is really positive. Now draw roots for the tree. Write in each root one thing that would help the positive thing to happen. Now draw leaves. In each leaf write how that positive change would affect yourself and others.

What makes a good role model?

AIM
Introducing the idea of being a good role model.

APPROXIMATE TIME
5–15 mins

EQUIPMENT REQUIRED
- paper
- pen

HANDOUTS NEEDED
What makes a good role model? (p.172)
Template 1: Values coins (p.189)

Values:

In Lead-in Exercise 1.1, the young person or group started to collect their values on coins. This exercise may help the participants identify positive values that they see in themselves and value in others.

Instructions
IN A ONE-TO-ONE AND GROUPWORK SETTING

1. Ask the participant(s):
    'Who do you look up to?'

2. This could be a family member, friend, teacher, sports coach, youth worker, etc. Encourage them to think of someone they know in preference to a celebrity figure.

3. Ask the young person to draw the outline of a person on the **What makes a good role model?** handout on p.172 (or use the Template 4 on p.192).

4. Discuss why they are a good role model and what qualities this person has with the participant(s) and then ask them to write the qualities they see in their role model on their drawing.

5. Ask:

    'What makes a good role model?'

6. Ask them:

    'Who looks up to you?'

7. Draw out of the participant(s) if they have anyone for whom they are a role model, e.g. a younger sister or brother.

8. Ask the young person to write the qualities they themselves have that make them a good role model onto the same figure.

Alternative exercise

APPROXIMATE TIME

5–15 mins

EQUIPMENT REQUIRED

- pens
- flipchart paper
- Post-it notes

HANDOUTS NEEDED

You could ask the participant(s) to write their role model's qualities on Post-its. Then using an outline of a person on a piece of flipchart paper, ask the participant(s) to put their Post-its on to the outline, who then acquires the qualities of a good role model. Ask the young person to write the qualities they themselves have that make them a good role model onto Post-its and place them on the same figure.

✓

WHAT MAKES A GOOD ROLE MODEL?

Think about who you look up to. Draw a picture of them. Write on it all the qualities that you like about them.

Add the qualities people who look up to you value in you.

FOLLOW-UP EXERCISE 4.7

What others think of me

AIM

To explore any issues of peer pressure and reputation in relation to the incident that led to the young person being placed on the course.

APPROXIMATE TIME

5–15 mins

EQUIPMENT REQUIRED

- pens (at least two colours)
- flipchart (optional)

HANDOUTS NEEDED

What others think of me (1) (p.176)
What others think of me (2) (p.177)

Instructions

IN A ONE-TO-ONE SETTING

1. Explain what a reputation is, and give an example.

2. Give the young person a copy of **What others think of me (1)** on p.176. Suggest that the young person consider what their own reputation is amongst their peer group, asking them to identify what their mates used to think of them before they committed a crime and what they think of them now.

3. Ask:

    'What would your mates have said if you hadn't committed the crime?'

4. Now ask:

    'Who most cares for you?'

5. Ask the young person:

    'What reputation have you got?'

    'What reputation would you ideally like to have?'

6. The young person can write down their thoughts first, or simply discuss them with the facilitator, whichever works best for them. The facilitator might like to read responses on a flipchart.

7. To help with this discussion, give the participant a copy of **What others think of me (2)** and ask them to circle the words that describe their reputation. Then ask them to circle the words that they would like to be associated with them in a different colour.

8. Ask the participant what they could do or change to attain the reputation that they would like.

IN A GROUPWORK SETTING

1. Explain what a reputation is, and give an example.

2. Give each participant a copy of **What others think of me (1)**. Suggest that the participants consider what their own reputation is amongst their peer group, asking them to identify what their mates used to think of them before they committed a crime and what they think of them now.

3. The young person can write down their thoughts first, or simply discuss them with the group, whichever works best for them.

4. Have a general discussion about reputations. Ask:
   'What would your mates have said if you hadn't committed the crime?'

5. Now ask:
   'Who most cares for you?'

6. Ask the participants:
   'What reputation have you got?'

   'What reputation would you ideally like to have?'

7. To help with this discussion, give each participant a copy of **What others think of me (2)** and ask them to circle the words that describe their reputation. Then ask them to circle the words that they would like to be associated with them in a different colour.

8. Ask the participants what they could do or change to attain the reputation they would like.

Extension/homework exercise

APPROXIMATE TIME
10 mins–½ hour

EQUIPMENT REQUIRED
- paper
- paints, crayons, coloured pencils, etc.
- fabric, coloured card, coloured tissue, etc.
- glue
- scissors (optional)

HANDOUTS NEEDED
none

The reputation the young person would like to have could be written artistically or drawn as a picture.

✓

WHAT OTHERS THINK OF ME (1)

Before committing crime:

How my mates *used* to think of me:

After committing crime:

How my mates think of me *now*:

If I hadn't committed the crime, my mates would have said:

WHAT OTHERS THINK OF ME (2)

Circle the words that describe your reputation.

Circle the words that describe the reputation you would like to have.

Reliable	Unreliable
Responsible	Irresponsible
Caring	Uncaring
Cool	Uncool
Liked	Not liked
Nice	Not nice
Strong	Weak
Bully	Victim

_____   _____

The Martians have landed!

AIM

To revisit and prioritize the values identified during the course.

APPROXIMATE TIME

15–30 mins

EQUIPMENT REQUIRED

- flipchart paper
- marker pens

HANDOUTS NEEDED

Template 1: Values coins (p.189)
Template 5: Anger cards (p.193)

If you and your participant(s) have successfully collected the gold coins comprising a set of values, you can all have a bit of fun with this exercise.

Instructions

IN A ONE-TO-ONE SETTING

1. Take out all the values coins that you have collected over the previous sessions. Write down on separate sheets of flipchart paper a statement which is the exact opposite of each value – one statement per sheet. We can imagine that these are laws imposed by the Martians.

2. Ask the young person to imagine living under those 'Martian' laws. You could say:

   'We are only really aware of our values when they are threatened or breached.'

3. Give the young person a pile of anger cards from p.192 and ask them to put them on the Martian laws that make them most angry. They can put more on laws that anger them more.

4. Now place each value coin over the Martian law that represents its opposite. The number of anger coins will indicate which law caused most anger, and therefore which value is most cherished. This should lead to a list of values in order of importance for the participant.

5. You could ask:

'What are values? Are they important?'

'If we all lived fully by these values, would life be better or worse?'

'Would we be happier?'

'Would crime occur?'

IN A GROUPWORK SETTING

1. Describe or create a scenario in which the Martians have landed (if you have a DVD player and monitor, perhaps you could use a clip of a popular movie to set the scene). Ask the group to be Martians, and help them to draw up Martian laws on sheets of flipchart paper on the floor (one law per sheet of paper). Each Martian law should breach or be the exact opposite of one of the values written on the gold coins, e.g. 'No one is allowed to protect the people they love', or 'Everyone has to lie all the time'.

2. Once all of the Martian laws have been drawn up, give everyone a number of 'anger cards'. You can use **Template 5: Anger cards** on p.193.

3. Ask the group now to imagine that they are ordinary humans trapped in a world that has been taken over by the Martians, and living under their laws. Read out the Martian laws one by one, and ask everyone to think for a moment about having to abide by these rules every day. Ask them to mill around reading the laws which are spread on the floor. Then distribute their anger cards according to those which make them most angry – they can put as many on one sheet as they like. They could grunt and make angry noises and comments about the laws as they do so.

4. The scenario changes and the Martians are beaten. You could say:
   'We are only really aware of our values when they are threatened or breached.'

5. Place the gold coins over the Martian laws, and put them into order, with the one that raised the most anger when breached at the top. This should lead to a list of values in order of importance for the group.

6. You could ask:
   'What are values? Are they important?'

   'If we all lived fully by these values, would life be better or worse?'

   'Would we be happier?'

   'Would crime occur?'

FOLLOW-UP EXERCISE 4.9

Looking to the future

AIM
To encourage the young person to look forward and make a commitment to avoid offending in future.

APPROXIMATE TIME
10 mins

EQUIPMENT REQUIRED
- pens
- flipchart paper
- pre-written list of options
- frame
- art materials
- photograph of the young person (optional)

HANDOUTS NEEDED
Looking to the future (p.183)

Instructions
IN A ONE-TO-ONE SETTING

1. Ask the young person to identify three actions needing to be taken to avoid hurting people through crime in the future.

2. Ideas may already have been generated from previous exercises (e.g. Follow-up Exercise 4.5: My harmony tree on p.167).

3. Most people who have been victimized are anxious to know that the person who hurt them will avoid doing the same thing to anyone else. If the person who was hurt has been contacted, they might like to know what the young person plans to do differently in the future.

4. If the young person is struggling for ideas, they could circle options from a list that you prepare for them, or create their own. You could also remind them of things they have said during the course that may be relevant.

5. The commitments could be written onto the three footprints on the **Looking to the future** handout from p.183 to represent the three steps they will take, or on a ladder or other graphic image.

6. To initiate a discussion, you could ask the following questions:

   'Where would you like to be in six months' time?'

   'What might the person you hurt like to hear about you in six months' time?'

   'Think about what you did and what you would do differently now.'

7. The three commitments can be written out neatly or illustrated. You could frame the commitments for the young person to keep, perhaps overlaying them onto a photograph of the young person (for example one taken when they are doing practical reparation).

8. Be clear with the young person that this is a voluntary commitment and not part of a contract (for example for a Referral Order). However it might be something that could be integrated into a supervision or intervention plan.

9. Decide with the young person whether they would find it helpful to review how well they are doing with their commitments, perhaps setting a date to look at them again in a few weeks or months.

IN A GROUPWORK SETTING:

1. Ask each young person to identify three actions needing to be taken to avoid hurting people through crime in the future. You can write up their ideas on flipchart paper.

2. Ideas may already have been generated from previous exercises (e.g. Follow-up Exercise 4.5: My harmony tree on p.167).

3. Most people who have been victimized are anxious to know that the person who hurt them will avoid doing the same thing to anyone else. If the person who was hurt has been contacted, they might like to know what the young person plans to do differently in the future.

4. If the young person is struggling for ideas, they could circle options from a list that you prepare for them, or create their own. You could also remind them of things they have said during the course that may be relevant.

5. The commitments could be written onto the three footprints on the **Looking to the future** handout from p.183 to represent the three steps they will take, or on a ladder or other graphic image.

6. To initiate a discussion, you could ask the following questions.

   'Where would you like to be in six months' time?'

   'What might the person you hurt like to hear about you in six months' time?'

   'Think about what you did and what you would do differently now.'

7. The three commitments can be written out neatly or illustrated. You could frame the commitments for the participants to keep, perhaps overlaying a photograph of the young person (for example one taken when they are doing practical reparation).

8. Be clear with the participants that this is a voluntary commitment and not part of a contract (for example for a Referral Order). However it might be something that could be integrated into a supervision or intervention plan.

9. Decide with each young person whether they would find it helpful to review how well they are doing with their commitments, perhaps setting a date to look at them again in a few weeks or months.

Extension exercise

APPROXIMATE TIME

5–10 mins

EQUIPMENT REQUIRED

* set of pictures of people in different careers

HANDOUTS NEEDED

You could ask:

> *'If you have children, what do you hope they will be when they grow up?'*

To get this discussion going, you could have a set of pictures for them to circle, showing, for example, a builder, youth worker, bus driver, young offender, doctor, father, mother, police officer, etc.

LOOKING TO THE FUTURE

Write or draw on to the footprints three steps that you are going to take to keep out of crime.

Explain restorative justice to someone new

AIM
To consolidate the young person's understanding of restorative justice.

APPROXIMATE TIME
5–10 mins

EQUIPMENT REQUIRED
- pens

HANDOUTS NEEDED
Explain restorative justice (p.186)

Instructions
IN A ONE-TO-ONE SETTING

1. Ask the young person to reflect back to you what 'restorative justice' is, as if they are speaking to someone who doesn't know what it is and has never heard the term – perhaps a young person who has just started the victim empathy course.

2. Give them the **Explain restorative justice** handout from p.186, and give them a few minutes to write down their initial thoughts.

3. Ask them:

    'So what's this restorative justice thing about again…?'

IN A GROUPWORK SETTING

1. Split the group into pairs. Ask the participants to discuss what restorative justice is, and to come up with a few sentences describing it, as if they are speaking to someone who doesn't know what it is and has never heard the term – perhaps a young person who has just started the victim empathy course.

2. Ask them:

    'So what's this restorative justice thing about again…?'

3. Give them the **Explain restorative justice** handout from p.186, and allow them a few minutes to write down their initial thoughts.

4. After a few minutes, ask the group to discuss their thoughts.

Extension/homework exercise

APPROXIMATE TIME

20 minutes–2 hours

EQUIPMENT REQUIRED

- paper
- pens
- coloured pencils, crayons, paints, etc.
- coloured paper, tissue paper, fabric, etc.
- glue
- scissors (optional)

HANDOUTS NEEDED

The young person could be encouraged to express their idea of restorative justice through the arts; in rap lyrics, a poem, artwork, creative writing or drama. This could be done individually, in pairs, or as an entire group.

✓

EXPLAIN RESTORATIVE JUSTICE

'So what's this restorative justice thing about again…?'

Module 4 Close and evaluation

AIM

To give the young person the opportunity to express how they are feeling and to evaluate the course.

Instructions

The material the participants have covered during this course may have left them with painful and difficult feelings. This should be acknowledged. Allow the young person to express their feelings and assist you in assessing whether they need to be doing any follow-up work. A planned post course interview with each participant would be helpful to achieve this.

Remind the young person of the support structure they have: community, family, friends, mentor, youth offending team officer, etc.

Ask the young person what they found most helpful and least helpful in the victim empathy programme, explaining that it will be useful to learn from them how the programme can be improved. Give the young person an evaluation questionnaire to fill in. In a groupwork setting this can become an excellent way to learn what has worked well, and what needs to be adapted or changed for future groups.

Thank the young person for their involvement.

The young person could create a 'Show and Tell' portfolio of the victim empathy course, perhaps to present to their Panel, to court, or to the person they hurt. They could present their apology letter in person to the person they hurt. Perhaps the young person could light a candle to represent all the people who have been victimized, and as a symbol of hope. Allow the young person time to speak, read anything they have written or show the creative works they have made. The young person could keep the portfolio.

Consider giving out an attendance (rather than achievement) certificate for the programme.

Victim Empathy Scale

Don't forget to repeat the Victim Empathy Scale if this was completed prior to the start of the course. The results (comparing the 'before' and 'after') can be used in sentence plan reviews or evaluations to inform risk assessments, providing you have the young person's consent. They can also indicate whether the course is of benefit and whether what you offered in the course works in affecting change.

Ongoing work

The Victim Empathy Scale can also indicate areas for ongoing victim empathy work. This course isn't necessarily complete in itself, and further work on victim empathy may be helpful or necessary. Consider following a groupwork experience with one-to-one work.

Restorative processes

Don't forget to follow up any potential for restorative work that emerges from the course, either directly or through the restorative justice worker or department in your organization.

TEMPLATE 1: VALUES COIN

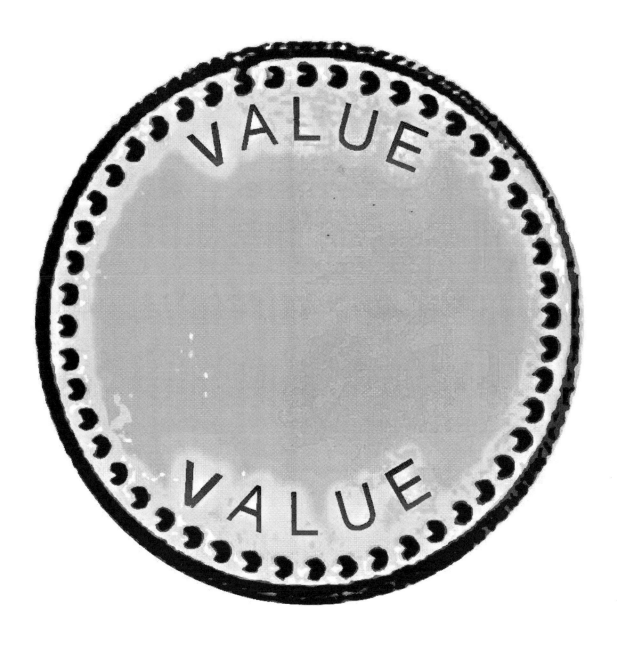

TEMPLATE 2 FEELINGS FACES

TEMPLATE 3: THOUGHT AND FEELINGS BUBBLES

✓

TEMPLATE 4: HUMAN FIGURE

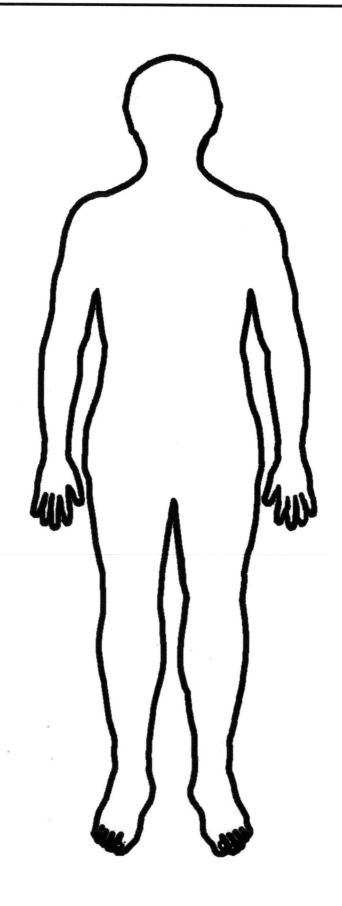

TEMPLATE 5: ANGER CARDS

EVALUATION

Please help to improve the course by writing on this page.

The thing I learned most from this module was:

The thing I learned most from the course so far was:

The thing I found most difficult/challenging about this module was:

The thing I found most difficult/challenging about the course so far was:

One thing I liked about this module was:

One thing I liked about the course so far was:

It would be good if you included…

Circle some words for how you feel now:

Satisfied	Helped	Challenged	Happy
Positive	Gutted	Depressed	Angry
Terrific	Hopeless	Confident	Negative
Questioning	Annoyed	Uncertain	Okay
Bored	Responsible	Interested	Upset
Confused	Great	Sad	Frustrated
Worried			

Pre- and post-victim empathy scales[5]

VES(V)
NAME:_____Date of birth:_____

READ EACH STATEMENT ON THE QUESTIONNAIRE AND PUT AN X AT THE
POINT ALONG THE LINE WHICH BEST DESCRIBES YOUR VIEW.

Thinking about the person involved, would you think they:

1. Were affected by what happened to them

_____
A great deal (A)   quite a lot (B)   not really (C)   not at all (D)

2. Lied about what happened to them

_____
Not at all (A)   a bit (B)   a lot (C)   totally (D)

3. Provoked you

_____
Absolutely (A)   mostly (B)   not really (C)   not at all (D)

4. Were responsible for what happened

_____
Absolutely (A)   mostly (B)   not really (C)   not at all (D)

5. Could have prevented what happened

_____
Not at all (A)   only with difficulty (B)   quite easily (C)   very easily (D)

6. Felt upset about what happened

_____
Felt very upset (A)   quite upset (B)   a little upset (C)   not upset (D)

_____
5   Beckett, R.C. and Fisher, D. (2009) Reprinted with kind permission.

7. Avoided doing things or going places because of what happened

| Not at all (A) | a bit (B) | a lot (C) | totally (D) |

8. Were left feeling unsafe because of what had happened

| Very unsafe (A) | quite unsafe (B) | a little unsafe (C) | not affected (D) |

9. Had got themselves into similar situations in the past

| Very possibly (A) | quite possibly (B) | unlikely (C) | very unlikely (D) |

10. Got off on the attention they received

| Very possibly (A) | quite possibly (B) | unlikely (C) | very unlikely (D) |

11. Were to blame for what happened

| Not at all (A) | slightly (B) | pretty much (C) | totally (D) |

12. Deserved what happened

| Absolutely (A) | mostly (B) | not really (C) | not at all (D) |

13. Felt afraid in the situation

| Felt very afraid (A) | felt quite afraid (B) | felt little fear (C) | felt no fear at all (D) |

14. Thought about the situation afterwards

| Very many times (A) | often (B) | occasionally (C) | never (D) |

15. Exaggerated what happened to them

| Very possibly (A) | quite possibly (B) | unlikely (C) | very unlikely (D) |

16. Worried about something similar happening again

| Almost certainly (A) | possibly (B) | unlikely (C) | very unlikely (D) |

17. Were left feeling violated (abused)

Very unlikely (A)   somewhat unlikely (B)   possibly (C)   very possibly (D)

18. Will make money in compensation out of what happened

Definitely (A)   Probably (B)   Maybe (C)   No (D)

19. Felt angry about what had happened

Extremely angry (A) pretty angry (B)   slightly angry (C)   not at all angry (D)

20. Will be able to forget about what happened

Very easily (A)   quite easily (B)   not easily (C)   Not at all (D)

21. Will be affected in the long term by what happened

Very unlikely (A)   somewhat unlikely (B)   possibly (C)   very possibly (D)

22. Felt victimized as a result of what happened

Very victimized (A) mostly victimized   slightly victimized   not at all victimized
                     (B)   (C)   (D)

✓

VES(P)

NAME:_____Date of birth:_____

READ EACH STATEMENT ON THE QUESTIONNAIRE AND PUT AN X AT THE POINT ALONG THE LINE WHICH BEST DESCRIBES YOUR VIEW.

Thinking about the person involved, would you think they:

1. Felt angry about what had happened

_____

Extremely angry (A)   pretty angry (B)   slightly angry (C)   not at all angry (D)

2. Will make money in compensation out of what happened

_____

Definitely (A)   probably (B)   maybe (C)   no (D)

3. Could have prevented what happened had they been more careful

_____

Not at all (A)   only with difficulty (B)   quite easily (C)   very easily (D)

4. Felt bad about what happened to them

_____

Felt very bad (A)   felt bad (B)   felt a little bad (C)   did not feel bad (D)

5. Were responsible for what happened

_____

Absolutely (A)   mostly (B)   not really (C)   not at all (D)

6. Thought about the situation afterwards

_____

Very many times (A)   often (B)   occasionally (C)   never (D)

7. Deserved what happened to them

_____

Absolutely (A)   mostly (B)   not really (C)   not at all (D)

8. Felt upset about what happened

_____

Felt very upset (A)   quite upset (B)   a little upset (C)   not upset (D)

9. Were left feeling unsafe because of what happened

Very unsafe (A)	quite unsafe (B)	a little unsafe (C)	were not affected (D)

10. Were affected in the long term by what happened

Very unlikely (A)	somewhat unlikely (B)	possibly (C)	very possibly (D)

11. Felt they had lost something important

Very possibly (A)	quite possibly (B)	unlikely (C)	very unlikely (D)

12. Could have taken more precautions to avoid what happened

Absolutely (A)	mostly (B)	not really (C)	not at all (D)

13. Were inconvenienced by what happened

Extremely (A)	a lot (B)	a little (C)	not at all (D)

14. Were worried about something similar happening again

Almost certainly (A)	possibly (B)	unlikely (C)	very unlikely (D)

15. Were affected by what happened to them

Absolutely (A)	mostly (B)	not really (C)	not at all (D)

16. Only lost material possessions

Definitely (A)	probably (B)	maybe (C)	unlikely (D)

17. Exaggerated what had happened to them

Very possibly (A)	quite possibly (B)	unlikely (C)	very unlikely (D)

18. Felt they were a victim as a result of what happened

very much (A)	quite a lot (B)	a little (C)	not really (D)

✓

19. Were left feeling violated (abused) as a result of what happened

Very unlikely (A)	somewhat unlikely (B)	possibly (C)	very possibly (D)

20. Lied about what happened to them

Not at all (A)	a bit (B)	a lot (C)	totally (D)

21. Were able to forget what had happened

Very easily (A)	quite easily (B)	not easily (C)	not at all (D)

22. Were to blame for what happened

Not to blame at all (A)	slightly to blame (B)	pretty much to blame (C)	to blame (D)

Score Key VES Violence

	A	B	C	D
1.	0	1	2	3
2.	0	1	2	3
3.	3	2	1	0
4.	3	2	1	0
5.	0	1	2	3
6.	0	1	2	3
7.	3	2	1	0
8.	0	1	2	3
9.	3	2	1	0
10.	3	2	1	0
11.	0	1	2	3
12.	3	2	1	0
13.	0	1	2	3
14.	0	1	2	3
15.	3	2	1	0
16.	0	1	2	3
17.	3	2	1	0
18.	3	2	1	0
19.	0	1	2	3
20.	3	2	1	0
21.	3	2	1	0
22.	0	1	2	3

Scoring and interpreting the results

When the young person has completed the questionnaire, work out their personal victim empathy score, which will be somewhere between 0 and 66. This should give you an idea of their level of victim empathy. Victim empathy as measured by the Victim Empathy Scale assesses the extent to which a client accepts responsibility and does not blame the person they hurt, and the degree to which they accept that the person they victimized has been harmed. In general terms, the lower the score the greater the level of empathy that the young person is showing. You can then use this grading system:

Score of 0 – 25   'a lot of empathy'
Score of 25 – 35   'some empathy'
Score of 35 – 66   'very little or no empathy'

Score Key VES Property

	A	B	C	D
1	0	1	2	3
2	3	2	1	0
3	0	1	2	3
4	0	1	2	3
5	3	2	1	0
6	0	1	2	3
7	3	2	1	0
8	0	1	2	3
9	0	1	2	3
10	3	2	1	0
11	0	1	2	3
12	3	2	1	0
13	0	1	2	3
14	0	1	2	3
15	0	1	2	3
16	3	2	1	0
17	3	2	1	0
18	0	1	2	3
19	3	2	1	0
20	0	1	2	3
21	3	2	1	0
22	0	1	2	3

Comparing the young person's score at the start and end of the programme should indicate whether the young person has developed more empathy as a result of the intervention.

The Victim Empathy Scales were piloted during 2009 with 59 young people from the Thames Valley who had committed a range of violent and property crimes (although the pilot wasn't related to involvement in a victim empathy programme). The rough grading system above was devised by comparing the raw scores from the Victim Empathy Scales with the clinical assessment of the young people's practitioners. The numbers were small, which should be taken into consideration when using the grading system.

It is relatively easy for you to collate your own data on the victim empathy levels of your client group. To develop this further, you may also like to assess their level of taking responsibility, which is another key theme in this course. To do this:

1. Remind yourself of the concept of empathy by reading 'What is victim empathy?' on p.10 and the concept of responsibility by reading Module 1: Thinking about what I did (p.36).

2. Use your own judgement to make an assessment of the level of empathy and responsibility of the young person, and mark it as 'a lot', 'some', or 'little/none'. Assign a value for each as follows:

    •   your assessment of empathy: a lot = 1, some = 2, little or none = 3

    •   your assessment of responsibility; a lot = 1, some = 2, little or none = 3

3. Meanwhile ask the young person to complete the appropriate Victim Empathy Scale, grade their victim empathy score as above, and assign the grade with a number as follows: a lot of empathy = 1, some empathy = 2, little or no empathy = 3.

4. Finally compare your own assessment with their victim empathy score, as indicated in Table 1.

Table 1: Calibrating the victim empathy grades by comparing them to your own assessment

Young person	Raw victim empathy score	Victim empathy grade	Your assessed level of empathy	Your assessed level of responsibility
James	18	A lot = 1	Some = 2	Some = 2
Sacha	41	Little or none = 3	Some = 2	Little or none = 3
Karl	26	Some = 2	A lot = 1	A lot = 1

This will allow you to fine tune the grading system, and may provide an insight into the accuracy of your own clinical assessment. It is worth noting that in the Thames Valley trial, professionals showed optimism in their assessments of empathy levels. This may be because young people who offend demonstrate an ability to empathize more generally but struggle to empathize with their own victim(s). Perhaps professionals also wish to show their clients in the best possible light and consequently over-emphasize the positive. In the Thames Valley results, young people damaging property demonstrated more empathy than those committing acts of violence, although this was not a statistically significant finding. Statistical analysis found a significant positive correlation between professionals' assessment of client empathy and responsibility taking. That is, professionals who assessed their clients as having higher levels of empathy tended also to assess their clients as having higher levels of responsibility.